Locomotives from
THE NATIONAL COLLECTION

Peter Waller and Alan C. Butcher

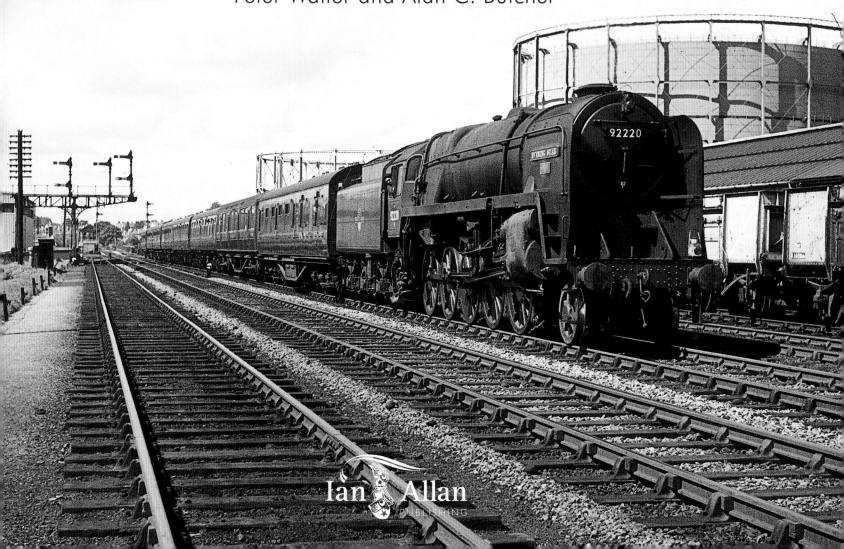

Ian Allan
PUBLISHING

London & North Eastern Railway No 4472 *Flying Scotsman*
Front cover: See page 50 for locomotive history. *Gavin Morrison*

Southern Railway No 34051 *Winston Churchill*
Back cover: See page 63 for locomotive history. *Hugh Ballantyne*

British Railway No 92220 *Evening Star*
Previous page: Developed from the earlier 'Austerity' design of 2-10-0, the Class 9F was to become the final of the 12 BR Standard classes to be built. Primarily produced for freight traffic where they excelled, for example, on the Tyne Dock–Consett iron ore trains, the first of the type emerged from Crewe Works in January 1954 and, in total, 251 were constructed by Crewe and Swindon works between then and March 1960 when the last of the class — No 92220 *Evening Star* — was completed. The completion of No 92220 marked the end of an era as it was the last main-line steam locomotive constructed for use on BR and, to mark the event, it was completed in green livery and fitted with a copper-capped chimney.

Although predominantly a freight locomotive, the class was also to see operation on passenger trains, with service over the much-mourned Somerset & Dorset Joint line being one example of the type's flexibility. Arguably the most successful of the BR Standard classes, the '9Fs' were destined to have a tragically short life, being withdrawn between 1965 and 1968, with many members of the class seeing less than a decade of main-line service. No 92220 was withdrawn in March 1965 after only five years' use. A further seven examples survive in private preservation, a number significantly influenced by those sold for scrap to Woodham Bros at Barry. On 25 August 1962 No 92220 *Evening Star* is pictured here, arriving at Bath with the 10.32am Saturdays Only service from Bournemouth to Bradford, which had travelled over the Somerset & Dorset line. *Hugh Ballantyne*

Acknowledgements
The photographs for this title have come from a number of sources and thanks are due in particular to Hugh Ballantyne, David Cross, John Edgington, Roy Hobbs, Derek Huntriss, Martin Jenkins, Rodney Lissenden, the late John McCann, Colin Marsden, Michael Mensing, Gavin Morrison, Bruce Oliver, Derek Penney, Norman Preedy, the late R. C. Riley, and Ron White of Colour-Rail.

First published 2008

ISBN (10) 0 7110 3304 4
ISBN (13) 978 0 7110 3304 5

Published by Ian Allan Publishing

an imprint of Ian Allan Publishing Ltd, Hersham, Surrey KT12 4RG.

Printed by Ian Allan Printing Ltd, Hersham, Surrey KT12 4RG

Code: 0810/D

visit the Ian Allan Publishing web site at:
www.ianallanpublishing.com

Introduction

Established in York in 1975, the National Railway Museum was and remains one of the constituent museums of the National Museum of Science and Industry, standing alongside the Science Museum in London and the National Media Museum in Bradford. Although the museum's current location is of relatively recent development, the antecedents of the collection stretch back almost to the dawn of the railway age itself.

It was in the mid-19th century when the Patent Office Museum, as forerunner to the Science Museum, acquired its first exhibits, which included *Agenoria*, sister to the *Stourbridge Lion* (one of the first steam locomotives in the USA), and the much-modified *Rocket*. Later in the 19th century, the North Eastern Railway, as successor to the pioneering Stockton & Darlington Railway, also started to preserve items, creating, within the walls at York, the first railway museum in the city. A number of these exhibits were later to appear at the S&DR's centenary exhibition in 1925. While other railway companies were perhaps not as active in preserving items of interest, a small number of non-NER exhibits were gradually to be added to the collection at York.

Although there was no co-ordinated effort to preserve the nation's railway heritage at this stage, a number of important locomotives were, however, to survive from the early years of the railway age. This was largely the result of either being sold for further use in industry or being used for some non-operational role within the railway industry. The survival of *Locomotion*, for example, following its withdrawal in 1841 was down to the fact that it was adapted for use as a stationary boiler, from which status it was rescued in 1857, making it one of the first locomotives to be formally preserved. For a number of years, *Locomotion* was displayed at Darlington Bank Top station in the company of another locomotive, Stockton & Darlington No 25 *Derwent*, which had survived for almost 30 years in industrial use prior to being preserved in 1898.

Preservation was on a fairly piecemeal basis through the early decades of the 20th century, with only the LNER having a proper museum as such, although the other 'Big Four' companies also started to put on one side notable locomotives and rolling stock. It was in the late 1920s that private preservation commenced with the purchase, by the Stephenson Locomotive Society, of the ex-LBSCR 0-4-2 *Gladstone*. Now part of the National Collection, *Gladstone* was a precursor for the boom in railway preservation that occurred from the early 1950s onwards. This expansion has seen the preservation of far greater numbers of locomotives and rolling stock than could ever have been envisaged in the formulation of a National Collection. However, preservation in these years was not guaranteed; shortly before the outbreak of World War 2, it was decided at the highest level that the final ex-NBR Atlantic — No 875 *Midlothian* — should be added to the LNER's collection. The locomotive, already withdrawn, was hastily restored to service but, following the outbreak of war, was again withdrawn and, with the pressing need for scrap, there was to be no second reprieve.

The greatest impetus for the creation of a national strategy for the acquisition and preservation of a representative selection of locomotives and rolling stock came in 1951, three years after the Nationalisation of the railway industry, following the completion of a report commissioned by the British Transport Commission, by the appointment of a new curator to look after the collection and to create a new museum in London. A schedule of potential acquisitions was also developed, essential in an era when rapid change was resulting in the disappearance of steam traction. During the 1950s the number of exhibits started to grow rapidly, resulting in items being stored in locomotive sheds across the country. In 1961, the new Museum of British Transport opened in a converted bus garage at Clapham. Apart from the railway exhibits, the museum also housed a number of trams and other road exhibits, reflecting the all-encompassing role of the BTC within the public transport industry.

By the mid-1960s it was becoming evident that the existing museums were not wholly suitable and, following the 1968 Transport Act, it was decided to create a new National Railway Museum in a converted roundhouse in York. The decision to base the new museum in York did not meet with universal support; there were many who took the view that a national museum needed to be based in London. Despite the vociferous opposition, work progressed on the development of the new museum and it was formally opened by HRH the Duke of Edinburgh in 1975. Since that date, the museum's collection has continued to grew — inevitably as the industry continues to develop and as the first generation of diesel and electric stock comes to the end of its career — and the museum itself has both expanded at York while also opening a second site — 'Locomotion' — located, appropriately, in Shildon. The decision to reduce the number of railway exhibits at the main Science Museum site in London has also resulted in more exhibits — such as the prototype *Deltic* — being transferred to the NRM.

Despite the increased space that developments at York and Shildon have offered, it is not possible to show the entire National Collection at the two sites and the NRM has always had a policy of placing locomotives and rolling stock on loan to other museums and preserved railways. Thus museums like 'Steam' in Swindon and the Bressingham Steam Museum play host to locomotives while some of the preserved railways have also seen locomotives on loan either for display or operation.

Over the years, many of the classic locomotives from the Collection have been seen at the head of specials on the main line. However, the increasing age of the locomotives featured as well as the need to preserve the historical integrity of them for future generations means that in the years to come fewer locomotives from the National Collection will be restored to an operational condition. One such stalwart — the only surviving 'V2' 2-6-2 *Green Arrow* — has just been taken out of service at the time of writing, at the end of its boiler certificate; now some 70 years old, it is unlikely that the locomotive will ever run again as major work will be required. The museum needs to balance the necessity for conservation with the desire to operate and, ultimately, the former will be the priority.

The National Railway Museum is now more than three decades old and, since it was opened in 1975, it has had to grow to reflect the evolving railway industry and, inevitably, this process will continue into the future. New exhibits will be added as they are withdrawn from service and there will undoubtedly continue to be a debate about the development of the collection and the space required to house it. With annual visitor figures of some 750,000, the National Railway Museum is one of the most popular tourist attractions outside London; as with all museums, however, it will need constantly to evolve and develop in order to keep attracting these levels of visitors. For all those interested in railways, we need to salute the prescience of the founding fathers and thank those who, over the years, have ensured that Britain possesses a National Collection of railway interest that is second to none.

Author's note
The National Collection now incorporates more than 100 locomotives as well as some 200 items of rolling stock; within an 80-page album it is not practical to try to illustrate every single locomotive, but an attempt has been made to reflect the variety held by the museum, from the earliest steam locomotives through to the most recent diesel and electric traction on display. Although every effort has been made to record the featured locomotives and stock in service or in early preservation, this has not proved possible in all cases and so, for some examples, more recent views are included.

Rocket

There are perhaps few more iconic steam locomotives in the history of railways than the 0-2-2 entered by George and Robert Stephenson, along with Henry Booth, in the Rainhill Trials held by the Liverpool & Manchester Railway between 6 and 14 October 1829, in which *Rocket* ultimately proved victorious (winning the then princely sum of £500). Although *Rocket* was not the first steam locomotive to be constructed, it was the first to incorporate a number of recent innovations — such as the use of a multi-tube boiler and a blastpipe — which marked a significant advance on those locomotives constructed earlier. On 15 May 1830, *Rocket* was one of the locomotives used for the opening of the Liverpool & Manchester Railway; driven by Joseph Locke, the locomotive was to knock down and kill William Huskisson, the MP for Liverpool, who thus became one of the first recorded fatalities of the railway age. In 1834, the locomotive was further modified, although the alterations were not successful.

Following service on the Liverpool & Manchester, *Rocket* passed to the private railway of Lord Carlisle in Cumbria. It was donated to the Patent Office Museum in London in 1862, although the locomotive as preserved is significantly different from that originally built by the Stephensons. In 1979, prior to the events to mark the 150th anniversary of the L&MR in 1980, a replica of the original locomotive was built. Shortly after its construction, the replica is seen here on a temporary track in Kensington Gardens, Hyde Park. The only obvious major external difference between this and the original locomotive is a slightly foreshortened chimney, a necessity given that clearances under bridges today are lower than in the 1820s as a result of the use of more ballast being used on the track.
Harry Luff/Online Transport Archive

Sans Pareil

In terms of early locomotive engineers, Timothy Hackworth was one of George Stephenson's main competitors and the two of them were among the contenders for the prize at the Rainhill Trials in October 1829. For the trials, Hackworth constructed an 0-4-0, *Sans Pareil*. This locomotive was less sophisticated technically than the Stephensons' *Rocket*, featuring a double return flue boiler rather than the more advanced multi-tube boiler featured on *Rocket*. The two cylinders of *Sans Pareil* were also installed vertically, which resulted in poor riding, while other problems — such as its weight, a breakdown and a loss of water — meant that the ultimate prize passed to the Stephensons.

Despite these problems, the Liverpool & Manchester Railway acquired *Sans Pareil* as well as *Rocket* and, later seeing service on the Bolton & Leigh Railway, *Sans Pareil* was ironically to have a longer main-line service than its more illustrious contemporary. Withdrawn by the B&LR in 1844, *Sans Pareil* was sold to Coppull Colliery, Chorley, where it was used as a stationary engine until it was presented to the Patent Office Museum in 1863. As with *Rocket*, a replica of *Sans Pareil* was constructed in 1979 prior to the 150th anniversary of the Liverpool & Manchester Railway. In order to mark the anniversary, cavalcades of locomotives were run at Rainhill over a weekend and the replica *Sans Pareil* is recorded there on 27 May 1980. *Gavin Morrison*

Stockton & Darlington Railway No 1 *Locomotion*

George Stephenson was born in 1789, the son of an engineman at Wylam Colliery, and it was at Wylam that he first encountered a steam engine when *Puffing Billy* was operated at the colliery in 1813. The following year, Stephenson built his first successful locomotive. Over the course of the next 10 years his involvement with the nascent railway industry grew, culminating in his appointment as engineer for the Stockton & Darlington Railway and the opening of the

first works in Newcastle of Robert Stephenson & Co in 1823. It was in this factory that *Locomotion* was completed in 1825 for use on the newly-completed S&DR. The original locomotives supplied to the S&DR were not wholly successful and it took Timothy Hackworth's 0-6-0 *Royal George*, completed in 1827, to prove that steam traction was ultimately reliable. In 1828, *Locomotion* suffered a boiler explosion, in which the locomotive's driver was killed. Restored to traffic and later rebuilt, *Locomotion* was to remain in

service until 1841 when it was converted into a stationary boiler. In 1857, it was preserved and initially placed on display in Alfred Kitching's workshops near Hopetown Carriage Works until 1892 when it was transferred for static display at Darlington Bank Top station, where it remained until 1975. It is currently displayed at the Darlington Railway Centre on loan from the National Collection. On 30 April 1965, *Locomotion* is seen on display at Darlington Bank Top station. *Gavin Morrison*

Stockton & Darlington Railway No 25 *Derwent*

Born in December 1786, Timothy Hackworth was one of the pioneers of the railway age and one of George Stephenson's main competitors in terms of the development of the steam locomotive. Following an early career working at collieries in the north east, he joined Robert Stephenson & Co at the company's Forth Street Works in 1824 and, while there, suggested that the driving wheels of *Locomotion* should be coupled. In 1825, he was appointed to take control of the Stockton & Darlington's locomotives

and machinery. He designed the first 0-6-0 in 1827 — *Royal George* — which was also the first locomotive on which the cylinders drove directly on to the wheels.

His *Sans Pareil* was one of the unsuccessful competitors at the Rainhill Trials and, during the 1830s, he maintained a relationship with the S&DR while also running his own independent locomotive-building business. During this time he improved his designs of locomotive, with a number of these later types being acquired by the S&DR. One of these was

No 25 *Derwent*, which was built to Hackworth's design by William and Alfred Kitching of Hopetown Works, Darlington. The locomotive was to remain in service on the S&DR until 1869 when it was then sold for industrial use on the colliery lines of Pease & Partners at Crook, County Durham. In 1898, it was again withdrawn and presented to the North Eastern Railway and was subsequently to be displayed for many years at Darlington Bank Top station, where it is seen on 30 April 1965, in the company of *Locomotion. Gavin Morrison*

Grand Junction Railway No 1868 *Columbine*
The GJR, stretching from Birmingham to the Liverpool & Manchester Railway, was one of the pioneering long-distance railways in the British Isles. Opened on 4 July 1837, the line was ultimately to become part of the London & North Western Railway and an integral link of the West Coast main line. In 1845, GJR No 49 was constructed at Crewe, one of the earliest locomotives to be built at the then relatively new works of the GJR. The Grand Junction was to merge with the L&MR and the London & Birmingham Railway in 1846 to become the LNWR, and No 49 was to be renumbered 1868 by the newly created railway. This classic locomotive is pictured here in the original York museum on 30 August 1959. *Colour-Rail*

Furness Railway No 3 *Coppernob*
As with a number of other relatively small railway companies, the first locomotives operated by the Furness Railway were supplied by outside contractors to the manufacturers' designs. In 1846, the then newly opened railway acquired two 0-4-0s from Bury, Curtis & Kennedy — Nos 3 and 4 — which were larger versions of the railway's first two

locomotives, which the same supplier had delivered two years earlier. Both 1846-built locomotives were to survive in service until withdrawn in 1898 with No 4 succumbing in January of that year and No 3 following in December. On withdrawal, No 3, nicknamed 'Old Coppernob', was placed on display on a stand outside Barrow station, where it was to remain for more than four decades before being

damaged by a German air raid in 1941. It was then transferred to storage at Horwich. Subsequently displayed at Clapham, the locomotive is seen here standing on the turntable within the new National Railway Museum on 10 July 1975, surrounded by other exhibits, including ex-Shropshire & Montgomeryshire Gazelle (see p28).
Gavin Morrison

London & North Western Railway
No 3020 *Cornwall*

In the 1840s, the railways were endeavouring to increase speed and, at the time, the most obvious means of achieving this was through the use of large single driving wheels. However, the larger the driving wheel, the greater the problem of the inter-relationship between boiler and axle. One solution to this problem was the Crampton design, whereby the axle for the driving wheels was located behind the firebox. Popular in Europe, a limited number were used on railways in Britain, including the London & North Western. However, in 1847, Francis Trevithick, the son of the pioneering Richard, designed a 4-2-2, *Cornwall,* with the intention of avoiding the long wheelbase inherent within the Crampton design. In order to achieve this, Trevithick designed the locomotive with a transverse channel at the top of the boiler through which the drive axle passed.

The locomotive thus completed, with its 8ft 6in driving wheels, was to be exhibited at the Great Exhibition of 1851. In 1858 the locomotive was virtually rebuilt completely — little more than the original frames were retained — as a 2-2-2 by John Ramsbottom. Apart from a further minor rebuild it remained in service in 1902 initially as LNWR No 173 before becoming No 3020 on the duplicate list in 1886. In 1907, the locomotive was reinstated for hauling an inspection saloon and remained operational on departmental duties until withdrawn and preserved in 1927. The scale of the single driving wheel is evident in this view of the locomotive.
Derek Penney

11

Wantage Tramway No 5 *Shannon*

When the Great Western main line was constructed to Brunel's plans in the late 1830s, the route bypassed the market town of Wantage, which resulted in the town being served by a station — Wantage Road — some 2½ miles distant. Eventually, following the passing of the Tramways Act of 1870, proposals were concluded for the construction of a branch between the main line and the town. Following construction, the line, which was initially horse operated, was opened in October 1875 although there had already been experiments with the use of steam. In early 1878, the tramway acquired a 0-4-0T primarily for freight traffic following the purchase of earlier steam tram engines for use on passenger services. This locomotive was numbered 5 and had been built in 1857 by George England & Co of New Cross in London for the Sandy & Potton Railway before passing to the LNWR (where the name *Shannon* originated).

Passenger services ceased over the still independent Wantage Tramway on 1 August 1925 and, following complete closure on 19 December 1945, the GWR acquired No 5 for £100 for overhaul and display. Initially, No 5 was displayed at Wantage Road station until the station itself was closed on 7 December 1964. For a period thereafter, the locomotive's future was uncertain before it was ultimately transferred to Didcot, becoming part of the National Collection. On 29 July 1984, the locomotive — the world's oldest surviving well tank — was recorded in front of the locomotive shed at Didcot, where it is on loan to the Great Western Society.
Hugh Ballantyne

Midland Railway No 158A

Matthew Kirtley, the son of a colliery owner, was appointed the first Locomotive Superintendent of the Midland Railway at the age of 31 in 1844, following a career that had seen him initially work as a fireman on the Warrington & Newton Railway gradually progressing to become Locomotive Superintendent of the Birmingham & Derby Junction Railway (the smallest of the three constituent companies of the MR on its formation). He was to hold the post until his death in 1873. On his appointment, he inherited a motley selection of locomotives and was at the forefront of encouraging the MR board to expand the railway's own workshops at Derby in order to be able to supply its own requirements.

During his period of office, he designed a number of highly successful locomotives, pioneering the use of the brick arch firebox and double 'sandwich' frames. Among the wheel arrangements that Kirtley favoured was the 2-4-0, which he used widely for both passenger and freight designs. Of the large number of this arrangement produced during Kirtley's reign, only one example — No 158A — survives. This locomotive, No 158 when new, was built at Derby in October 1866 but was to be significantly rebuilt twice during its career — in December 1881 and in June 1897. It was renumbered 158A in the MR's duplicate list in August 1896, becoming No 2 in October 1907. Fewer than 250 of Kirtley's 2-4-0s passed to the LMS in 1923,

and of these, only a few were still in service at the end of the decade, including No 2. The survivors had 20000 added to their running number during the 1930s, with No 2 becoming No 20002. In 1930, sister locomotive No 1 was restored to its MR condition as No 156A but this preservation was to be short-lived and the locomotive was scrapped in September 1932. No 20002 was one of a handful of the 2-4-0s to survive World War 2 and, on withdrawal in July 1947, was restored to MR livery as No 158A. It is pictured here while on loan to the Midland Railway Centre at Butterley. *Harry Luff Collection/ Online Transport Archive*

South Devon Railway *Tiny*
Always the maverick, Isambard Kingdom Brunel promoted the use of the broad gauge — 7ft 0¼in — on the railways for which he was the engineer. Among these lines was the South Devon Railway from Exeter to Plymouth with its associated branches. Although originally designed on the atmospheric principle, the problems associated with this form of traction resulted in its quick abandonment and the rapid adoption of conventional steam power. Among the locomotives acquired by the South Devon Railway was *Tiny*, a 0-4-0 vertical boiler locomotive constructed by Sara & Co in 1868. Following the Great Western Railway's acquisition of the SDR on 1 February 1876, *Tiny* became GWR No 2180 until it was withdrawn in 1883. Following withdrawal, it was retained at Newton Abbot to power machinery in the workshops that existed adjacent to the station until 1927, when this work ceased and the locomotive was preserved. For many years, this sole survivor of the broad gauge was on display at Newton Abbot station, as seen here on 5 September 1962. More recently the locomotive has been displayed at Buckfastleigh in the museum of the South Devon Railway Trust.
Colour Rail

14

North Eastern Railway No 66 *Aerolite*

For the Great Exhibition of 1851, Kitson & Co built a locomotive named *Aerolite* for display. This locomotive passed to the North Eastern Railway but was to be destroyed in an accident in 1868. The following year a replacement, again named *Aerolite*, was completed, and, like the original, was used by the NER to haul an inspection saloon. As originally built in 1869, the locomotive was a 2-2-2WT but, in 1886, the locomotive was to receive side tanks. It was also around this date that the locomotive was officially numbered 66. In 1892, the locomotive underwent a further rebuild, emerging as a 4-2-2. A further rebuild, in 1902, saw it converted into a 2-2-4T and it was in this form that the locomotive passed into LNER ownership in 1923. Classified X1 by the LNER, No 66 retained its original NER number post-Grouping and was one of only four 2-2-4Ts to pass to the new company — all of which had originated from the NER. Withdrawn in 1933, the locomotive was preserved as part of the LNER's museum collection and displayed at the original railway museum at York, where it is seen on 20 April 1954. *Colour-Rail*

15

Great Northern Railway No 1

With a career as Locomotive Superintendent of the GNR stretching from 1866 until 1895, when he died in office aged 75, only 11 days after he had been asked to resign, Patrick Stirling was one of the most influential engineers of his period. Although by the end of his period of office, the locomotives that he had designed were proving to be inadequate as the weight of trains increased, his earlier work had been highly successful. It was under Stirling that the famous 'Plant' Works at Doncaster constructed its first locomotives and among the earliest types to emerge was a batch of 4-2-2s. The first of these to be completed, and appropriately numbered 1, appeared from Doncaster Works — as the 50th locomotive built there — in April 1870. By the time that construction of the type ceased in December 1885 no fewer than 41 had been completed. Designed for use on express passenger trains, the class was fitted with 8ft 1in driving wheels. They were withdrawn between 1899 and 1912 and, following withdrawal in September 1908, No 1 was preserved. During 1908 the locomotive was displayed along with GNR Atlantic No 1442 at the Franco-British Exhibition held at White City, London. Restored to operational condition in 1938, it worked special services for a number of years. It is seen here on display at Doncaster Works on 18 June 1978 during an exhibition held to mark the 125th anniversary of the Works' opening.
Peter Waller

London & South Western Railway
No 298 (30587)

Born in 1804, James Beattie was one of the pioneering generation of locomotive engineers. Involved with the London & Southampton Railway, predecessor of the London & South Western, he was appointed Locomotive Superintendent of the latter in 1850, holding the post until his death in 1871. During his years in office, Beattie witnessed the considerable expansion of the LSWR and, in order to cater for services on the suburban lines around London, he developed, from 1856 onwards, a number of 2-4-0 well-tank designs. Following Beattie's death, he was succeeded by his son W. G., who held the position until 1878. Initially, he ordered further locomotives to his father's designs, including, in August 1873, a further batch of 2-4-0WTs. These locomotives were

delivered by Beyer Peacock between April and June 1874. Although the majority of these new locomotives were used to supplement those already in service in London, one, No 298, was sent new to the West Country and, as the type was supplanted from London suburban services, others followed, with a number being rebuilt.

Three of the class — Nos 298, 314 and 329 — were transferred to the Wenford Bridge branch in Cornwall in the mid-1890s and, following the withdrawal of the remainder of the type, were the only examples to survive into the 20th century. Initially, it was expected that newer locomotives would replace them but, with their short wheelbase, the trio was well-suited to working this freight-only line. It was not until 1962 that these locomotives were replaced by ex-GWR 0-6-0PTs. Two of the three have been

preserved including BR No 30587 as part of the National Collection. Originally LSWR No 298, it was built by Beyer Peacock in June 1874 and was rebuilt in 1889. Renumbered 0298 in the LSWR's duplicate list, it became E0298 following the Grouping and No 3298 in May 1933. The three survivors were designated Class 0298. Following withdrawal on 2 December 1962, the locomotive was stored before being transferred to Buckfastleigh for static display at the Dart Valley Railway in 1978. Shortly after official withdrawal, Nos 30585 and 30587 headed a 'Beattie Farewell' railtour on London suburban lines and the pair is pictured here at Hampton Court prior to running round the train for the return journey.
Roy Hobbs

North Eastern Railway No 1275

Sir Thomas Bouch was both one of the most successful of the mid-Victorian railway engineers and also, following the collapse of the first Tay Bridge (which was built to his design) in 1879, one of the most controversial. Subsequent to an early career that involved work with a number of early railway companies, he set himself up as a general engineer in the early 1850s and gained considerable work in both England and Scotland before his ill-fated scheme for crossing the Firth of Tay. One of his clients was the Stockton & Darlington Railway and, for the company, he designed the '1001' class of 0-6-0 for use on the railway's numerous mineral trains.

The first batch of six was manufactured by Gilkes, Wilson & Co of Middlesbrough following an order placed in 1852 and, despite merger with the North Eastern Railway in 1863, production of the type continued through to 1875. Only one example of the class — No 1275 — survived to pass to the LNER in 1923; quickly withdrawn, the locomotive was restored — albeit retaining the Worsdell boiler fitted in 1906 — for the Stockton & Darlington Centenary before being preserved in the original York museum. No 1275 was built by Dübs & Co of Glasgow in May 1874 and, prior to the reboilering of 1906, had been previously reboilered in 1883 and again in June 1896.

The locomotive spent the latter part of its career allocated to Malton shed where it was used to haul freight trains over the North Yorkshire Moors to Whitby. The locomotive is pictured here in the new National Railway Museum, York, on 6 May 1975, shortly after the museum was opened.

Gavin Morrison

North Eastern Railway No 901

On the creation of the NER on 31 July 1854, Edward Fletcher was appointed the new company's first Locomotive Superintendent. In 1872, he introduced the first of his '901' class of 2-4-0, which was designed to provide more powerful locomotives for express work. A total of 55 of the class were built between then and 1882, with Gateshead Works building 35 and the remainder being divided between Beyer Peacock & Co and Neilson & Co. As the weight of trains increased from 1885 onwards the class was often used to double-head expresses and, from the late 1880s, the arrival of more powerful classes saw them reallocated away from these services.

Withdrawal of the class commenced before World War 1 and only 10 examples survived into LNER ownership. Classified E6 by the LNER, the last of the type was withdrawn in July 1925; however, No 910, which had been based at York, was included in the procession to mark the centenary of the Stockton & Darlington Railway held that year and was subsequently preserved. In August 1975, celebrations, including a cavalcade, were held at Shildon to mark the 150th anniversary of the Stockton & Darlington Railway and a number of exhibits from the National Collection, including Gateshead-built example No 910, made the trip to County Durham. No longer capable of being steamed, No 910 was coupled to another ex-LNER locomotive for the cavalcade on 31 August. *Gavin Morrison*

London, Brighton & South Coast Railway
No 82 *Boxhill*

Following a 17-year career that had started under Daniel Gooch on the Great Western Railway, William Stroudley was appointed Locomotive & Carriage Superintendent of the LBSCR in February 1870. In the 20 years that he was in charge at Brighton, before his untimely death in France in December 1889, Stroudley was responsible for a number of classic locomotive designs. Of these the most notable was perhaps the diminutive 'A1' class 'Terrier' 0-6-0T, the first of which was completed in September 1872. The LBSCR required a powerful but lightweight suburban tank locomotive capable of operating with reasonable acceleration over the lightly laid tracks that formed its network in the London area. Stroudley had already designed small 0-6-0Ts for the Highland Railway and he adopted a similar approach for the LBSCR. Following experience with the first six, a further 44 slightly modified locomotives were constructed between 1874 and 1880.

By 1900, however, the traffic requirements of the LBSCR had changed and the decision was made to withdraw the majority of the class; although it was initially anticipated that the withdrawn locomotives would be scrapped — as indeed happened to 11 of them — the vast majority of those withdrawn were to see second-hand service on a variety of lines, from the Isle of Wight to the northwest of England. A number of the survivors on the LBSCR were rebuilt after 1911 with larger boilers and extended smokeboxes, these being reclassified as 'A1X'. A total of 16 of the original 50 survived to Nationalisation, including two that had ended up in Great Western ownership. The final examples were withdrawn by the end of 1963 with the closure of the Hayling Island branch.

No fewer than 10 of the 'A1' and 'A1X' classes survive in preservation with the National Collection's No 82 *Boxhill* being one of only two of the 'unrebuilt' examples. No 82 was built at Brighton Works in August 1880, being later renumbered 682. In March 1905, the locomotive was converted to a 2-4-0T as part of the LBSCR's trial for auto-train working, remaining in this condition until converted back to a 0-6-0T in 1913. One of only two 'A1s' still owned by the LBSCR at Grouping, No 682 was transferred to departmental stock for use at Brighton Works where it was renamed *Loco Works Brighton* and renumbered 380S in 1932. Finally withdrawn in August 1946, it was restored to LBSCR livery the following year and preserved. During the late 1950s a number of items for the future National Collection were stored at the former NER shed at Tweedmouth, and *Boxhill* is seen there in 1957. *Colour-Rail*

London, Brighton & South Coast Railway
No 214 Gladstone

The last design of express passenger locomotive by Stroudley during his years at the LBSCR was the Class B 0-4-2. The 36-strong type was produced to cope with the heavier loads then being operated over the line but within the restraints of utilising the existing turntables and permanent way. In order to achieve this, Stroudley took an earlier 0-4-2 design and modified it with larger 6ft 6in driving wheels. The first was completed at Brighton Works in 1883 with the remaining 35 being built between 1884 and 1891.

The entire class was named after contemporary politicians or people connected with the railway industry. One of the class — No 189 Edward Blount — was a medal winner at the 1889 Paris Exhibition and it was during his trip to France to see the locomotive on trial with the Paris, Lyons & Mediterranean Railway that Stroudley contracted the cold that led to his death in Paris.

From 1906 onwards, the majority of the class were fitted with new larger boilers, with most losing their names at the same time. Although withdrawals of the unmodified examples had commenced in April

1910, the bulk survived to be taken over by the Southern Railway in 1923, with the last of the class withdrawn in 1933. The pioneer of the type, No 214 Gladstone, was withdrawn in the 1927 and was initially secured for preservation through the efforts of the Stephenson Locomotive Society — the first main-line steam locomotive to be privately preserved, for the princely sum of £140 (the price included restoration to LBSCR livery) — before ultimately becoming part of the National Collection.
Derek Huntriss

North Eastern Railway No 1463

In the period following the resignation of Alexander McDonnell in 1884 and prior to the appointment of Thomas Worsdell in 1885, the position of Locomotive Superintendent of the NER was held briefly by the railway's then General Manager, Henry Tennant. Under his stewardship an urgent need for a powerful express locomotive arose as a result of inadequacies with McDonnell's '38' class 4-4-0s. The result was the '1463' class of 2-4-0, which was effectively a modified version of the earlier '901' class designed by Fletcher (see p19). With construction split equally between Gateshead and Darlington works, 20 locomotives were completed during 1885. In order to cope with the increasing weight of the East Coast expresses, the locomotives were often used to double-head trains with the '901' class. However, the type's career on East Coast expresses was relatively short as new 4-4-0s started to displace them following Worsdell's appointment. All 20 passed to the LNER in 1923; re-designated Class E5, the entire class was withdrawn between 1926 and February 1929. Gateshead-built No 1463 was preserved by the LNER and is pictured here in the new National Railway Museum in York, on 6 May 1975, shortly after the museum was opened. *Gavin Morrison*

Lancashire & Yorkshire Railway *Wren*

In 1887, the LYR completed its new locomotive works at Horwich. This vast site, which occupied some 81 acres, was served by a network of 18in gauge railway that was used for the movement of components around the works. In order to operate this network, a total of eight narrow gauge 0-4-0STs were constructed. The first three were built by Beyer Peacock with the later five being constructed in Horwich Works itself. The Beyer Peacock-built examples were delivered in 1887 while the later five followed between 1891 and 1901. The first of the octet were withdrawn in 1930 and, by 1948, only one example — *Wren* — remained operational. Following withdrawal in 1962, *Wren* was acquired for the National Collection. Horwich Works ceased locomotive building in 1962 with wagon and carriage repair undertaken thereafter until closure of all but the foundry in 1982. *Wren* is seen here in the old Clapham museum on 23 January 1965 in the company of two trams, including Douglas Head Marine Drive No 1, and a horse-bus. *Gavin Morrison*

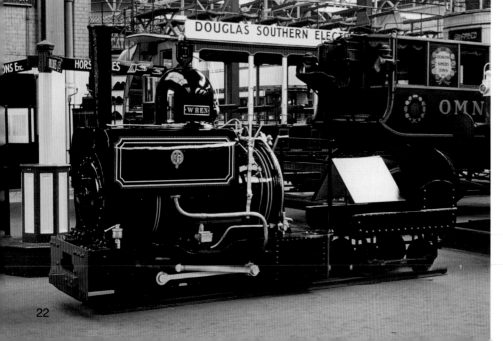

Great Western Railway No 2516

Appointed Locomotive, Carriage & Wagon Superintendent of the GWR in 1877, William Dean was to hold the position for 25 years until his retirement in 1902. During this period, which saw the GWR finally eliminate the broad gauge, he produced a number of classic designs, including the 0-6-0 'Standard' or 'Dean Goods'. The first of the 260-strong class emerged in 1883 with production continuing until 1899. Of those built, 20 were later rebuilt as 2-6-2Ts. A number of the class were requisitioned for War Department use during both world wars; those transferred to the WD between 1917 and 1921 were generally returned, but many of those sent overseas in World War 2 were never repatriated. In total, 232 of the class were still in service at the Grouping in 1923, but this number had been significantly reduced to only 54 by Nationalisation. Withdrawal was rapid thereafter with only one example — No 2516, built at Swindon in March 1897 — in service at the end of 1955. Following withdrawal in May 1956, the locomotive was added to the National Collection and is the only example of the class to survive in preservation. No 2516 is seen here at Swindon Works, four years after withdrawal. *Colour-Rail*

Lancashire & Yorkshire Railway No 1008

John Aspinall, who was later knighted, was appointed Chief Mechanical Engineer of the LYR in 1886. It was under Aspinall that the reputation of the railway, previously regarded as one of the more backward of the large regional railway companies, dramatically improved as his locomotive designs proved successful. It was in February 1889 that the first of his 2-4-2Ts — No 1008 — emerged from Horwich Works (the first locomotive to be completed at the LYR's new workshops). Designed primarily for passenger services, these 'Radial Tanks' operated widely over the LYR network, including both branch and main-line services. For the latter, they were fitted with a special design of water pick-up equipment to facilitate the use of water troughs when operating in either direction.

Following Aspinall's promotion, his successors, Henry Hoy and George Hughes, perpetuated the design, with 330 being constructed by 1911. Hughes modified the design in 1912 to include a Belpaire firebox and a number of the earlier locomotives were rebuilt with this feature. A total of 110 of the 'Radial Tanks' — including one originally sold to the Wirral Railway in 1921 — passed to BR in 1948, but withdrawal was rapid from the early 1950s. The last was withdrawn from service in 1960. The pioneer of the class — No 1008 — which had become LMS No 10621 in 1923 and BR No 50621 at Nationalisation — was preserved after withdrawal in September 1954 and is the only example of the type to survive in preservation. Restored to LYR livery, No 1008 stands outside the museum at York, on 29 April 1977. *Gavin Morrison*

Great Eastern Railway No 490

Born in Kent in 1837, James Holden had had considerable experience as a locomotive engineer before his appointment as Locomotive Superintendent of the GER in 1885. It was a position that he was to hold until 1907 when he resigned to be succeeded by his son. His first design for the GER was the 'T19' class 2-4-0 in 1885 and, in 1891, the first of a new class of 2-4-0s for cross-country mixed-traffic operation emerged from Stratford Works. Classified 'T26' by the GER and 'E4' by the LNER following the Grouping, a total of 100 locomotives were constructed between then and 1902. Numbered 1407-1506 by the GER, the locomotives received an 'E' suffix at Grouping before being renumbered 8407-8506. Between 1926 and 1940, 82 of the class were withdrawn, with the survivors being renumbered 2780-2797 in 1946 and thus 62780-62797 at Nationalisation in 1948.

Although a handful had been transferred for a period during the 1930s for operation on the Stainmore line between Darlington and Penrith, for which they had been fitted with side-window cabs at Doncaster, the class eked out its final years in service over the rural lines of Cambridgeshire. Withdrawal of the remaining 18 commenced in 1954 and only one example — No 62785 — survived into 1959. On withdrawal in December of that year, this locomotive (originally GER No 490) was preserved. It is recorded here on Cambridge shed on 20 May 1957. *R. C. Riley*

London & North Western Railway
No 790 *Hardwicke*

In 1863 the LNWR introduced, to the design of John Ramsbottom, its first 2-4-0; these were the first passenger locomotives produced for the LNWR to feature coupled driving wheels. The 2-4-0 design was perpetuated by Ramsbottom's successor, Francis Webb, who produced two new designs in 1874 — the

'Precursor' and 'Precedent' classes — to be followed by the 'Improved Precedent' class in 1887, and the 'Waterloo' class two years later. A total of 166 'Improved Precedents' was constructed between 1887 and 1901, of which 80 were to pass to the LMS in 1923. The surviving locomotives were renumbered between 5000 and 5079, with the last of the class being withdrawn in 1934. Originally No LNWR No

790, *Hardwicke* became No 5031 at Grouping. The locomotive was built at Crewe in 1892 and withdrawn in 1932. Preserved on withdrawal, No 790 is the only one of the LNWR's numerous 2-4-0s to survive in preservation. In late 1974, the locomotive in LNWR livery, stands outside the shed at Carnforth having been restored for operation on the main line.
Derek Huntriss

North Eastern Railway No 1621

Appointed Locomotive Superintendent of the NER in 1890, Wilson Worsdell took up the position that had previously been held by his brother. He occupied the post for 20 years during which time he designed the first 4-6-0 for use on an English railway. His first design for an express passenger locomotive for the NER was the Class M1 (later Class M) 4-4-0, of which 20 were built at Gateshead Works between 1892 and 1894. They were designed for use on East Coast main line expresses and featured in the

'Railways Races' of 1895 when the rival East and West Coast companies competed for the fastest trains to Aberdeen. The class was modified between 1903 and 1908 and again between 1914 and 1929 when superheated boilers were fitted. All of the class passed to the LNER in 1923 where they were classified D17/1; the broadly similar NER 'Q' class 4-4-0, of which 30 were built in 1896-97, was designated 'D17/2'.

By the 1920s, the class had been largely supplanted on East Coast duties and, apart from one

casualty condemned as a result of an accident, withdrawals of the remaining 49 examples commenced in 1931. Two 'D17/1s' and seven 'D17/2s' survived World War 2, although both of the former were withdrawn in 1945. Of these No 1621 — a number which it had held throughout its career under both the NER and LNER — was selected for preservation and transferred to the museum in York. The locomotive is seen at the north end of York station on 19 March 1978. *Gavin Morrison*

London & South Western Railway No 563

Appointed in 1878 to succeed W. G. Beattie as Locomotive Superintendent of the LSWR, William Adams held the post until his retirement in 1895. Having already designed a number of 4-4-0 classes for the company, faced by the increasing weight of trains in the 1880s following the introduction of bogie coaches, Adams introduced four new classes of more powerful 4-4-0. These included the 20-strong 'T3' class built at Nine Elms Works between December 1892 and November 1893. Numbered 557-576, the class was primarily employed on express services until displaced by later designs produced by Adams' successors. All 20 of the class survived through to the Grouping in 1923 when they were renumbered E557-E576. Withdrawals commenced in 1930 but, despite this, No 563 (the 'E' prefix had been lost in 1933) underwent a general overhaul in 1935.

Stored in late 1938 and withdrawn the following March, No 563 was reinstated as a result of the outbreak of war and continued in service until 1945 when it was again withdrawn. Stored at Eastleigh along with other locomotives destined for the scrapyard, No 563 was selected in 1948 for display within an exhibition marking Waterloo station's centenary. Over the next decade No 563 was to be stored at a variety of locations, including a brief period at Tweedmouth, before being placed on display at the museum established at Clapham in 1961. In 1975, following the closure of the Clapham site and the concentration of the National Collection at York, No 563 was placed on display at the new museum. The locomotive, which is the only survivor of the class, is recorded here during the decade prior to its transfer to Clapham. *John McCann*

Shropshire & Montgomeryshire Light Railway
No 1 *Gazelle*

The S&MLR was one of a number of railways whose existence was influenced by the king of light railways in Britain — Holman F. Stephens. The original line, which ran northwestwards from Shrewsbury, had opened in the 1860s and, after a precarious existence, had closed in the 1880s. Following the 1896 Light Railways Act, Stephens was involved in a number of projects to revive or build light railways throughout much of the country. One of the lines that he revived was the erstwhile Potteries, Shrewsbury & North Wales Railway. Following reconstruction, the line reopened in 1911 and, in order to provide motive power, Stephens acquired a number of second-hand locomotives. These included a 2-2-2WT built in 1896 by Alfred Dodman & Co of King's Lynn. Originally owned by William Burkitt, a Norfolk seed merchant, the locomotive, fitted with passenger accommodation, had travelled widely over the network before being sold to the S&MLR.

On the S&MLR it was used in its original condition on the Criggion branch before being sent to W. G. Bagnall & Co for rebuilding as a 0-4-2T. It continued thereafter to provide the motive power for the Criggion branch, normally coupled to an ex-London County Council horse tram. Derelict by the early 1930s — passenger services over the branch having ceased in 1932 — the locomotive was again rebuilt in the late 1930s. In 1941, the War Department requisitioned the railway and its rolling stock in connection with the opening of a number of munition dumps and *Gazelle* found a new lease of life hauling early morning inspection trains. Transferred to the Longmoor Military Railway in 1950, it was put on display there, and later at the now-closed Museum of Army Transport at Beverley. Believed to be the smallest standard gauge steam locomotive ever constructed, *Gazelle* is pictured here, while on display at Longmoor, on 28 September 1968. *Gavin Morrison*

London & South Western Railway No 245

In 1895, Dugald Drummond was appointed Locomotive Superintendent of the LSWR in succession to William Adams. The first design of locomotive that Drummond produced for his new employers was the 'M7' class 0-4-4T. This class, which totalled 105 built between 1897 and 1911, was designed primarily for use on the intensive suburban services that the LSWR operated in and around London, although a number were also allocated to the West Country when new. Of the locomotives built,

95 were constructed at Nine Elms with the final 10 being built at Eastleigh. The last 50 were fitted with longer frames than the first 55 locomotives and were initially classified as 'X14', but all were eventually to be known as 'M7s'. In 1912, a number were fitted with a rudimentary system for push-pull use, which was upgraded during the 1930s using a compressed-air system. This equipment could only be fitted, however, to the longer-framed examples.

As a result of electrification, many of the class were transferred to operate branch lines in southwest

England. All but two of the 105 built passed to BR in 1948. Withdrawals began in 1957 and the final examples were withdrawn in 1964. Apart from LSWR No 245 — which became No 30245 at Nationalisation and is pictured here shortly after withdrawal at Fratton shed in June 1963, and which survives in the National Collection — there is one other member of the class in preservation. This is No 30053, which is now based on the Swanage Railway, having been repatriated from the USA. *Bruce Oliver*

Taff Vale Railway No 28

The TVR was one of the main competitors of the Great Western Railway in the valleys of South Wales, where it constructed a network of lines to the north of Cardiff to serve the once-enormous coal industry of the region. A total of 275 ex-TVR locomotives were absorbed by the GWR on 1 January 1922; of these more than 200 were 0-6-2Ts, including 14 Class 01s designed by Tom Hurry Riches, the Locomotive Superintendent of the TVR from 1873 until his death in 1911. The 0-6-2T type had been used elsewhere in Britain, but it was Riches who pioneered its use in South Wales. Built at Cardiff Works in 1897, No 28 was, like the remainder of the class, not to survive in GWR ownership for long, being withdrawn in October 1926, and all had gone by the end of 1931.

No 28 (as GWR No 450), however, was sold to the War Department following withdrawal and was to spend many years based at the Longmoor Military Railway in Hampshire where it was numbered 70205 and named *Gordon*. Withdrawn from military service in January 1948, a third career beckoned as the locomotive passed to the newly-created National Coal Board and it was transferred to South Hetton Colliery, part of the NCB's Durham No 2 Area. It was to remain in northeast England until withdrawal for the third time, whereupon, in January 1962, it was donated to British Railways and moved to Caerphilly Works for eventual restoration. Pictured still in its NCB livery, No 28 is recorded here in Caerphilly Works on 24 March 1963. *Colour Rail*

Great Northern Railway No 990 *Henry Oakley*
Following the 30-year period of Patrick Stirling, Henry Ivatt was appointed Chief Mechanical Engineer of the GNR in March 1896. A detailed examination of the railway's main line was undertaken by him, on foot, from which he came to the conclusion that, if he had known the state of the track before, he would not have accepted the position. He therefore instituted both improvements to the line and the development of more powerful locomotive types capable of handling the heavier trains operating at the end of the Victorian age. In May 1898, the first 4-4-2 Atlantic

locomotive built for operation on a British railway — No 990 — emerged from Doncaster Works. Nicknamed 'Klondyke' after the 1896 Klondike gold rush of 1896, the locomotive was to be named *Henry Oakley* after a former General Manager of the GNR in June 1900. A further 21 of the type were built — designated Class C1 by the GNR and 'C2' by the LNER after 1923. Although the class was reasonably successful, the performance of the 'C1s' was enhanced when they were later fitted with superheated boilers, No 990 being so treated in December 1922.

All 21 of the class passed to the LNER in 1923 with *Henry Oakley* being renumbered 3990. Withdrawn in October 1937, the locomotive was transferred to the LNER's museum at York in January 1938. In 1953, the locomotive was restored to steam for a double-headed special from King's Cross run to mark the centenary of Doncaster Works. The locomotive is pictured here with the other preserved ex-GNR Atlantic, No 251, as they prepare to depart from King's Cross with the centenary special to Doncaster on 20 September 1953. *John McCann*

Midland Railway No 673

Matthew Kirtley was succeeded as Locomotive Superintendent of the MR by Samuel Johnson, who held the position for 30 years through to his retirement in 1903. It was under Johnson that the MR's locomotives were painted in red rather than the olive green used previously. Under Johnson and his successors, the MR developed a 'small locomotive' policy, preferring either to operate, when necessary, double-headed or a more frequent service. Towards the end of the 19th century, in the era of the 'Railway Races to the North', the highest speeds were obtainable through the use of the largest diameter of driving wheel and the apogee of this type of locomotive were the various classes of 4-2-2 produced around the turn of the century. The first of Johnson's 4-2-2s, which became known as 'Spinners', emerged from Derby Works in June 1887 and between then and 1900, 95 were constructed for the MR. In November 1896 the first of the '115' class, with its 7ft 9in driving wheels, was completed. Eventually, this class was to number 15 locomotives with No 118 being completed in February 1897. Rebuilt in 1907 and renumbered 673 in the same year, the locomotive was one of 43 MR singles to pass to the LMS on 1 January 1923. No 673 was the last of the type to remain in service and, on withdrawal in 1928, was preserved. It is seen here in May 1980. *Derek Huntriss*

Great Northern Railway No 1247

Introduced by Henry Ivatt in August 1897, the Class J13 (LNER Class J52) represented a development of Stirling's earlier design of 0-6-0ST. Regarded as the GNR's standard shunting locomotive, a total of 264 were constructed for the railway between 1868 and 1909 with a number of the earlier Stirling type — designated Class J53 by the LNER — being later fitted with domed boilers so that they became virtually indistinguishable from the Ivatt design. The rebuilt

Stirling locomotives were classified 'J52/1' while the 85 Ivatt-designed locomotives became 'J52/2'. Ten of the 'J52/2s' were constructed by Robert Stephenson & Co and 25 — including No 1247 — by Sharp Stewart & Co.

No 1247 was completed in May 1899 and was initially renumbered 4247 at Grouping, becoming No 8846 under the LNER's 1946 renumbering scheme. All the Ivatt locomotives survived to pass to BR in 1948, although the first example was withdrawn

in August 1953 and they were all withdrawn by March 1961. Following withdrawal in May 1959, No 1247 (as BR No 68846) was privately preserved by Captain W. G. Smith, eventually becoming part of the National Collection. Restored to original GNR livery, the locomotive is seen here on 14 April 1962 shunting its train at Welwyn Garden City prior to heading to Hatfield with the Stephenson Locomotive Society's 'Seven Branch Lines' tour. *Roy Hobbs*

London & South Western Railway No 120

Nicknamed 'Greyhounds', the 66 members of the LSWR Class T9 4-4-0s were renowned for their sleek lines and ability to travel at speed. Designed by Dugald Drummond, the class followed on from his less-successful 'C8' class and, having learnt the lessons from this earlier design, the new engines were fitted with a larger boiler. The first of the 'T9s' emerged from Nine Elms Works, where 35 were built in June 1899, with a further 31 completed at the Glasgow works of Dübs & Co. From 1912 onwards, the class was fitted with superheaters — a policy introduced by Drummond's successor Robert Urie. Designed primarily for use on express services in the West Country, all 66 examples survived into the BR era but withdrawals started in 1951. All were withdrawn by the end of 1960 although No 30120 — originally LSWR No 120 — was selected to become part of the National Collection. The locomotive, withdrawn from Exmouth Junction shed, was overhauled at Eastleigh Works and restored to original LSWR green livery for the operation of special trains. Between March 1962 and late 1963 No 120 was a regular performer on main-line specials and is seen here running between Banbury and Woodford Halse double-heading a railtour with 'U' class 2-6-0 No 31790. *M. Mensing*

South Eastern & Chatham Railway No 737

Harry Wainwright became Chief Locomotive Engineer of the SECR in 1899, following the creation of the joint committee between the South Eastern and London, Chatham & Dover railways, and between then and his retirement in 1913 he produced a number of standard designs for the new company. The first of his 'D' class 4-4-0 locomotives, appeared in 1901. Eventually a total of 51 was constructed between then and 1907. Of these, 21 were rebuilt between 1921 and 1927 by Maunsell as the 'D1' class while 48 examples in total passed to British Railways at Nationalisation.

Withdrawals commenced in 1950 and, by the end of 1955, all of the original 'D' class had gone with the last of the 'D1s' withdrawn in 1962. Following its withdrawal in October 1956, No 31737 — built originally as SECR No 737 at Ashford Works in November 1901 — was preserved. This locomotive had initially become No A737 at Grouping, being subsequently renumbered by the Southern as No 1737. It is the only member of the class to survive in preservation and it has been restored to the highly elaborate dark green livery created for the SECR by Wainwright as seen at Ashford on 20 June 1960. *R. C. Riley*

Great Northern Railway No 251

In December 1902, Henry Ivatt introduced the first of his new and larger design of 4-4-2 for the Great Northern Railway, No 251, and, between then and August 1908, a total of 94 locomotives of this type were constructed. Fitted with larger boilers than the original GNR Atlantics, the locomotives were also designated 'C1' by the GNR, a classification retained by the LNER after 1923. As with the earlier design,

the larger locomotives were also to be fitted with superheaters during their career. All 94 passed to the LNER at Grouping, but withdrawals commenced in early 1944 and only 17 locomotives survived to pass to BR in 1948. Of these, only two actually carried their BR number and the class was completely withdrawn by November 1950. No 251, renumbered 3251 by the LNER in 1923 and allocated the number 2800 under the 1946 renumbering scheme (but never

carried), was withdrawn in July 1947 and transferred to the LNER's museum at York. Like No 990 — see p31 — the locomotive was restored to operational condition and used on the centenary special for Doncaster Works in 1953. Resplendent in original GNR Apple Green livery, the locomotive stands on display at the Doncaster Works open day on 20 July 1984. *Hugh Ballantyne*

Midland Railway No 1000

Under Samuel Johnson — and particularly during the time of his successor, Richard Deeley — the Midland Railway was one of a number of British railway companies to experiment with the concept of compound valve gears. However, it was only the Midland that persevered with its use as it suited the company's policy of running frequent and light trains. The first five compound locomotives, built to Johnson's design, emerged from Derby Works between January 1902 and November 1903.

Numbered 2631–2635 originally, the locomotives became Nos 1000-1004 with the MR renumbering scheme of 1907, retaining the numbers at Grouping. Under Deeley, a further 40 locomotives, ultimately Nos 1005-1044, were completed by March 1909. Deeley had taken Johnson's original concept and had simplified it so that the locomotives always started off in simple mode before switching to compound working once in motion.

The original five Johnson locomotives were rebuilt by Deeley's successor, Henry Fowler, between

November 1914 and December 1918. All were to survive to Nationalisation in 1948, although only four were to carry their allocated BR numbers. By now renumbered No 41000, the original No 2631 was withdrawn from service in November 1951. Towards the end of the decade, the locomotive was fully restored and reinstated to service on 13 June 1959 for use on special workings, before being transferred initially to the museum collection at Clapham. It is recorded here at Nottingham Victoria station on 11 September 1960. *Gavin Morrison*

Great Western Railway No 3440 *City of Truro*
Although William Dean pioneered the use of the 4-4-0 on the GWR, it was his successor — George Jackson Churchward — who was to produce the final locomotives of this type for the GWR, and also one of the most famous locomotives of all time in No 3440 *City of Truro*. Built at Swindon with double frames, the 20 locomotives of the 'City' class were similar to the designs produced by Dean. Of these, 10 were brand-new locomotives built in 1903 while the other 10 were rebuilds from the earlier 'Atbara' class of 4-4-0,

converted between 1902 and 1909. No 3440 was the 2,000th locomotive to be completed at Swindon Works, but its primary claim to fame comes from the fact that, on 9 May 1904, it became the first steam locomotive to be recorded officially running at more than 100mph when it achieved a purported 102.3mph descending Wellington Bank.

The locomotives were renumbered 3700-3719 in 1912. All 20 of the class survived through to the mid-1920s, but withdrawals began in 1927 and the last was withdrawn in 1931. When withdrawn in 1931,

No 3717, as it was then numbered, was preserved and displayed at the original railway museum in York until 1957. It was then restored to main-line service bearing its original number, 3440, for use on both enthusiast specials and regular trains from Didcot shed over the Didcot, Newbury & Southampton line. This second lease of life was to end in 1961. On 17 April 1960 the veteran 4-4-0 is pictured at Old Oak Common in the company of another classic preserved locomotive, the ex-Caledonian Railway 'Single', No 123. *R. C. Riley*

Great Eastern Railway No 87

During their periods as Locomotive Superintendent of the GER, James Holden and his successors introduced five designs of 0-6-0T locomotive to the railway with a total of 249 being built from 1886 onwards. All were constructed with 4ft 0in driving wheels. Holden's GER Classes R24 and S56 — later LNER Classes J67 and J69 respectively — were outwardly similar in appearance although the former was designed primarily for freight traffic and the latter for suburban passenger services out of London Liverpool Street station. Of the two designs, 160 were built at Stratford Works between 1890 and 1904 with the 'J69s' possessing slightly larger tanks and fireboxes. During the history of the type a number were rebuilt from 'J67' to 'J69' and vice versa.

From the original 160, 134 passed to BR ownership in 1948 with withdrawals of both types having commenced in 1940. Withdrawals began again in 1953 and by 1961 only 11 examples of the 'J69s' remained in service, all being condemned by the end of the following year. GER No 87 — renumbered 7087 at Grouping, 8633 under the LNER renumbering scheme of 1946 and thus 68633 on Nationalisation — was preserved following withdrawal in December 1960. The locomotive was built at Stratford Works in September 1904 and is pictured here having been restored to GER blue livery in December 1961, posed between the reservoirs near Copper Mill Junction, Stratford. *Roy Hobbs*

Great Eastern Railway No 1217E

Between 1900 and 1911, 90 0-6-0 freight locomotives were built for the Great Eastern Railway as Class G58 at Stratford Works, to the design of James Holden. The first 59, introduced in 1900, were built with round fireboxes and were classified 'J16' at the Grouping; these were all converted to 'J17' format with Belpaire fireboxes by 1932. The last 31 were built with Belpaire fireboxes from new and became Class J17 in 1923. The locomotives were originally GER Nos 1150-1239, receiving an 'E' suffix at Grouping before being renumbered 8150-8239. Under the 1946 LNER renumbering scheme, the locomotives were renumbered 5500-5589 with the exception of No 8200, which had been destroyed in 1944 as a result of damage from a German rocket during World War 2. The other 89 members of the class remained in service until 1954 when withdrawals commenced. By the end of 1961 only 12 of the class were left in service and all had been withdrawn by the end of the following year. One of the last to survive was No 65567 — originally GER No 1217 built in May 1905 — which was withdrawn in August 1962 and was preserved. Seen on 31 March 1962, towards the end of its operational life, No 65567 stands at Thetford having brought the RCTS's 'Great Eastern Commemorative' railtour over the line from Norwich via Swaffham. *Roy Hobbs*

North Eastern Railway No 1

Following the NER's decision to electrify the suburban network on Tyneside, it was also decided to electrify the steeply-graded line that ran from Trafalgar Yard, near Manors East station, to Newcastle Quayside. Although the line was only about a mile in length, it passed through three tunnels, which caused problems with ventilation, and there was also the possibility of fire caused by sparks from steam locomotive chimneys. In order to operate the newly-energised line, two Bo-Bo locomotives —

Nos 1 and 2 — were built in 1905 by Brush at Loughborough acting with British Thomson-Houston. They were fitted with both a bow collector (later replaced by a pantograph) and third-rail pick-up shoes; the former for use in the yards and the latter in the tunnels. Electric services were introduced in June 1905 and both locomotives survived through Grouping in 1923 and Nationalisation in 1948, retaining their original identities until renumbered 6480 and 6481 respectively under the LNER 1946 scheme, and then 26500/26501 by BR. Unclassified

until 1945, they were then designated as Class ES1. The Quayside line was dieselised in early 1964 and the two electric locomotives were withdrawn formally in September 1964. No 26501 was scrapped in 1966 but, following a period of store, No 26500 was preserved in 1968. Pictured here with Heaton DMU depot in the background, No 26500 stands alongside its sister locomotive towards the end of their career.
Colour-Rail

Great Western Railway No 2818

George Jackson Churchward was appointed Locomotive, Carriage & Wagon Superintendent of the GWR in 1902 in succession to William Dean. One of the most influential of all British locomotive engineers of the early 20th century, he revolutionised GWR locomotive design and, through his adoption of standardised boilers and other equipment, was to set the pattern for British steam locomotive practice thereafter. Noted for designing the first Pacific locomotive to operate on a British railway — No 111

The Great Bear of 1908 — Churchward was also to produce the first 2-8-0 to see service in Britain when, in June 1903, No 97 — later renumbered 2800 — was released from Swindon Works. The locomotive, designed for heavy freight operation, proved successful and production of further examples of the type commenced in 1905. By 1912, when the last of the class was completed at Swindon, a total of 83 had been built; a further 84 examples, with the design slightly updated by Collett as the '2884' class, were also built between 1938 and 1942. All passed to BR

in 1948 and it was not until 1958 — when the original No 2800 was withdrawn — that the class saw its first casualties. They had all had been withdrawn by 1965 with No 2818 — built at Swindon in 1905 — becoming part of the National Collection following withdrawal in October 1963. Apart from No 2818, six examples of the '2800' class and nine of the later '2884' type also survive in preservation. Withdrawn almost a year earlier, No 2818 is recorded here in store at Swindon in the late summer of 1964.
R. C. Riley

Great Western Railway No 4003 _Lode Star_

While recognising the need for improved locomotives for the GWR's main express services, Churchward undertook considerable research before ultimately designing the class of locomotive that was to be regarded as his masterpiece — the 'Star' class 4-6-0. In order to gain experience of contemporary Continental practice, he imported three French-built compound locomotives and designed his simple own four-cylinder 4-4-2, No 40, to compare performance. Experience with the two types convinced Churchward that the complexities of the compound design were such that he preferred the latter and a further 10 of

the locomotives were ordered for delivery in 1907, but as 4-6-0s rather than as Atlantics. No 40 was converted to a 4-6-0 in November 1909.

Between 1907 and 1923, a total of 72 examples, Nos 4001-4072 (No 40 had been renumbered 4000), were completed at Swindon Works. Following Churchward's retirement in December 1919 — he was killed later in the same month when he was hit by a train — his successor, Charles B. Collett, further developed the 4-6-0 design as his 'Castle' class — see p49 — and 15 of the 'Star' class, including the original No 4000 _North Star_ and the 10 completed in 1922/23, were subsequently

rebuilt to form part of the later class. Of the 58 remaining , the first examples were withdrawn in 1932 and only 47 passed to BR in 1948. Withdrawals were rapid thereafter with only eight examples still in service by the end of 1952 and the last was withdrawn in October 1957. On withdrawal in July 1951, No 4003 _Lode Star_, built at Swindon in February 1907, was preserved and is the only example of the class to survive. After withdrawal, the locomotive spent some time in store in Swindon Works and it is recorded here, on 16 June 1957, in the Stock shed there. _R. C. Riley_

London, Tilbury & Southend Railway
No 80 *Thundersley*

Thomas Whitelegg, appointed in 1880, was the first Locomotive Superintendent of the LT&SR and he held the post for 30 years. For passenger services over the line he designed a number of 4-4-2Ts, the last of which was a batch of four — LT&SR Class 70 — built by Robert Stephenson in May and June 1909. A further 35 of the class were constructed between 1923 and 1930. The second of the original batch was No 80 *Thundersley*. Displayed at the Franco-British Exhibition at White City when new, for which it was temporarily named *Southend*, the locomotive passed with the LT&SR to the Midland Railway in 1912, being renumbered 2177, the identity it retained until 1947 when it was renumbered 1966. In 1935, the locomotive was ornately decorated to mark King George V's Silver Jubilee. It became No 41966 at Nationalisation and, when withdrawn in June 1956, was the last of the original quartet to remain in service. Following withdrawal the locomotive was preserved and is the only example of the type to survive. On 11 March 1956, shortly before withdrawal, the locomotive, restored to LT&SR livery, hauled an RCTS special, the train is seen here at Bethnal Green. *R. C. Riley*

Great Central Railway No 102

Appointed Locomotive & Marine Engineer of the GCR in 1900 and Chief Mechanical Engineer two years later, John George Robinson oversaw the development of GCR locomotive design from then through to the Grouping of the railways in 1923. In 1911 he introduced the first of his '8K' class of 2-8-0 of which 130 were constructed between then and 1920. A further 18 of the later '8M' class were converted to Class 8K after the Grouping and a further 521 similar locomotives were constructed for use by the Railway Operating Division of the Royal

Engineers in World War 1. Of the total built, the LNER, which classified them as 'O4', acquired the original 130 examples plus 273 of the ROD-operated locomotives. A number of the class were subsequently rebuilt by the LNER after 1944 to the design of Edward Thompson, being classified 'O1' thereafter, and there were several variants between the unrebuilt ex-GCR locomotives as well.

Of those inherited by the LNER in 1923, a total of 329 passed to BR in 1948 with all being withdrawn by the end of 1966. GCR No 102 was built at Gorton Works in January 1912, being renumbered 5102 at

Grouping. Following the 1946 LNER renumbering scheme it became 3601 and thus BR No 63601 at Nationalisation. One of the 'O4/1' class of locomotives, No 63601 retained a small GCR Belpaire firebox and was thus close to the original design, albeit, as with the rest of the class, having been fitted with a Gresley chimney during the 1930s. The locomotive was withdrawn in June 1963 and is here recorded towards the end of its main-line operational life at Frodingham New Yard on 13 May 1961. This is the only known colour image of the sole member of the class to survive in preservation. *Colour-Rail*

Great Central Railway No 506 *Butler-Henderson*
Amongst the passenger types that Robinson
designed for the GCR was the 'Improved Director'
class of which 11 were built between December 1919
and December 1922 by the railway's own workshops
at Gorton. The first of the class to be completed was
No 506 *Butler-Henderson*. Designated Class 11F by

the GCR, these 11 became Class D11/1 at 1923 with
a further 24 of the type completed post-Grouping
being designated 'D11/2'. Initially, No 506 was
renumbered 5506 by the LNER but, under the 1946
renumbering scheme, was to become No 2660 and,
thus, No 62660 at Nationalisation in 1948. All the
GCR-built examples of the class were withdrawn in

1960, with No 62660 succumbing in October that
year before passing into preservation. It is the only
member of the class to survive. In August 1950
No 62660 is seen at Stainforth & Hatfield station at
the head of an RCTS special. *Colour-Rail*

North Eastern Railway No 901 (63460)

Designed by Sir Vincent Raven, the first of the NER three-cylinder Class T3 0-8-0s, No 901, was to emerge from Darlington Works in October 1919. Designed for freight work, the first example proved well capable in trials of handling the heavy coal and iron ore trains, but the initial five built by the NER were unpopular with locomotive crews, who disliked the maintenance and lubrication required for the centre cylinder. It was only after the Grouping in 1923 that the LNER authorised the construction of a further batch of 10 locomotives, which emerged from Darlington Works between March and May 1924. Although primarily designed for use on the heavy iron ore trains from Tyne Dock to the steelworks at Consett, six of this second batch were initially allocated to either York or

Hull. All the class was eventually to be based at Tyne Dock for use on the Consett trains.

Classified Q7 by the LNER, the original quintet retained their NER numbers (901-905) after 1923, with the 1924-built examples becoming Nos 624-6/8-34. Following the 1946 LNER renumbering scheme, the 15 became Nos 3460-3474. All passed to BR ownership in 1948 and remained in service until November and December 1962 when all were withdrawn with Class 9F 2-10-0s taking over their duties. The first of the class, by now renumbered 63460, was preserved as part of the National Collection. The locomotive is pictured here on 28 September 1963, after official withdrawal, heading the joint RCTS/SLS 'North Eastern' railtour south of Brancepeth. *Roy Hobbs*

London & North Western Railway No 9395

Destined to become the LNWR's main type of freight locomotive, the company's first 0-8-0 was designed by Webb and built at Crewe in 1892. By the time that the LNWR was subsumed into the LMS in 1923 a total of 572 locomotives with this wheel arrangement had been constructed. Of these the last variant to be built was the 'G2' class designed by Hewitt Pearson Montague Beames, who was appointed the Chief Mechanical Engineer of the LNWR in December 1920. The first of the 'G2s' — No 485 — emerged from Crewe Works in November 1921 and 60 were completed between then and October 1922. A number of earlier locomotives were rebuilt with the higher-pressure boiler fitted to the

'G2s' from 1936 onwards and were classified 'G2a'. At the Grouping in 1923, No 485 became No 9395 with all 60 of the 'G2s' passing both to the LMS and, ultimately, BR in 1948. Withdrawal of the type began in 1959 and all were condemned by the end of 1964. By now renumbered 49395, the first of the class was withdrawn in November 1959 and was preserved; it is the only one of the ex-LNWR 0-8-0 designs to survive. For many years the locomotive was displayed at the Ironbridge Gorge Museum in an unrestored condition but it has subsequently been fully restored to working order. The locomotive stands in withdrawn condition at Uttoxeter in this May 1960 view. *D. H. Beecroft/ Colour-Rail*

North Staffordshire Railway No 2

The only ex-NSR steam locomotive to survive in preservation is 'L' class 0-6-2T No 2, which, although constructed at the railway's Stoke Works after the Grouping of 1923, was built mainly to a design of John Henry Adams, the NSR's Locomotive Superintendent between 1902 and 1915, albeit slightly modified by his successor, John Albert Hookham. Under the ownership of the LMS, the locomotive was renumbered 2271 but was destined to have a relatively short main-line career, being withdrawn in November 1937 — one of the last of the class to survive — before being sold for industrial use at Manchester Collieries, where it was named *Princess*. Towards the end of its career, by now in the ownership of the National Coal Board, the locomotive was repainted in NSR livery for display in 1960 and, following withdrawal by the NCB, was preserved in 1967. The locomotive is recorded here at Manchester Collieries in August 1964. *John Edgington*

Great Western Railway No 4073 *Caerphilly Castle*

In January 1922 Charles B. Collett succeeded George Jackson Churchward as the CME of the GWR. Churchward had been a pioneer in the development of standardised locomotives and his successor, faced by the need to replace locomotives inherited from the companies that the GWR had absorbed at the Grouping as well as for more powerful motive power, maintained a similar policy. The first of Collett's designs to appear, in August 1923, was 4-6-0 No 4073 *Caerphilly Castle*. Fitted with a larger boiler than the earlier 'Star' class (see p43), the new design also featured a larger cab that

offered greater protection from the elements to the footplate crew. With a tractive effort of 31,625lb as opposed to the 'Star' class's 27,800lb, the new design was, when completed, the most powerful passenger locomotive then in operation on any British railway.

As with another of the iconic locomotives of the era, LNER No 4472 *Flying Scotsman*, No 4073 was displayed at the British Empire Exhibition at Wembley in 1924 and, in comparative trials afterwards, was to prove slightly superior to the Gresley design. In all, a total of 179 'Castle' class locomotives were constructed between 1923 and 1950, all being built

by Swindon Works, of which 16 were rebuilt from earlier designs. The class was hugely successful seeing operation on both passenger and freight traffic across the GWR network. Following the introduction of the replacement diesel-hydraulic locomotives from the late 1950s, mass withdrawals of the 'Castle' class commenced in 1959 with the final examples being withdrawn in 1964 and 1965. No 4073 had been withdrawn in May 1960, and was transferred by road for display in the Science Museum. On 20 May 1956, some four years prior to withdrawal, No 4073 stands in steam at Old Oak Common. *R. C. Riley*

London & North Eastern Railway
No 4472 *Flying Scotsman*

Undoubtedly one of the most famous steam locomotives in the world, No 4472 *Flying Scotsman* is a relatively recent acquisition for the National Collection, having been preserved privately when originally withdrawn in January 1963. However, No 4472 was not the first of the 'A1' class Pacific locomotives designed by Sir Nigel Gresley; that honour went to Great Northern Railway No 1470 *Great Northern*, which was built at Doncaster in 1922 which was only the second non-tank Pacific to be built in Britain following the GWR's *Great Bear* of 1908. This class was designed to provide the additional power required to haul the heavier passenger trains of the period. The earlier GNR locomotive designs, most notably the Ivatt Atlantics (see pp31/36), had been severely taxed as the weight of trains increased and Gresley had already proved the potential of six-coupled locomotives with his 'H4'

class of 2-6-0s (which were later classified 'K3' by the LNER). Influenced by contemporary US design, the new locomotive and the second of the type, No 1471 *Sir Frederick Banbury*, soon proved themselves on the East Coast main line. The result was that the GNR ordered a further batch of 10, of which the first was No 1472 *Flying Scotsman*, which were delivered shortly after the Grouping in 1923. Soon renumbered 4472, the locomotive was selected for display at the Empire Exhibition at Wembley alongside GWR 'Castle' class No 4073 *Caerphilly Castle*. Following comparative tests with the GWR locomotive, the 'A1' design was slightly modified and a further 40 locomotives of the type were delivered in 1924 and 1925.

All of the class, with the exception of 20 built by the North British Locomotive Co in Glasgow (Nos 2563-2582), were constructed at Doncaster. Between 1927 and 1948, the class, with the exception of *Great Northern*, were fitted with higher-

pressure boilers and reclassified A3. A further 27 of the 'A3' type were built new between 1928 and 1935. The class proved highly successful on the East Coast main line and, despite the arrival of the streamlined 'A4' class, continued to dominate the route. In the late 1950s, a number of the 'A3s', including No 60103 (as *Flying Scotsman* had been renumbered by BR) underwent further modification with the fitting of a double chimney and German-style smoke deflectors. On withdrawal in January 1963, No 60103 was purchased for preservation by Alan Pegler and, provided with a second tender. The locomotive continued to operate on the main line even after the end of BR steam operation in August 1968 until the early 1970s. Thereafter the locomotive spent a period in the USA and visited Australia, although subsequently its financial position was increasingly insecure. The locomotive was acquired by the National Collection in 2004. *Derek Cross*

London, Midland & Scottish Railway No 4027
The Midland Railway had long adopted the use of 0-6-0 locomotives for freight traffic when Henry Fowler introduced the first of his Class 4 goods locomotives, No 3835, in October 1911. A total of 192 of the class were constructed between then and the end of 1922 and, on the creation of the LMS in 1923, the type was adopted as the new company's standard freight locomotive, with a further 580 being built between November 1924 and March 1941. The first of these was No 4027, which was completed at Derby Works. Apart from Derby, locomotives of the class were also constructed at Crewe, St Rollox and Horwich, as well as by outside contractors. All the 580 LMS-built examples passed to BR in 1948 and none was taken out of service until 1959. However, as steam was eliminated from the BR network, the Class 4F rapidly diminished, with only 11 examples remaining in service in 1965. All of were withdrawn by the end of that year. Following withdrawal in November 1964, No 4027 — by this date renumbered 44027 — was preserved; it is one of three LMS-built examples to survive. (One of the original MR-built 0-6-0s is also preserved.) On 3 October 1982, No 4027, restored into LMS livery, arrives at Swanwick Junction with a service from Butterley at the Midland Railway Centre.
Hugh Ballantyne

Southern Railway No 777 *Sir Lamiel*

An Irishman by birth, R. E. L. Maunsell was appointed Chief Mechanical Engineer of the South Eastern & Chatham Railway in November 1913. At the Grouping in 1923 he became CME of the new SR, a post that he held until 1937. The SR had an immediate need for a design of large express passenger locomotives capable of handling 500-ton trains at an average speed of 55mph, which ultimately became the 'Lord Nelson' class, but as a stop-gap measure, Maunsell was authorised to produce an improved version of Urie's earlier 'N15' class 4-6-0 for use on the South Western main line out of Waterloo. The 'King Arthur' class eventually totalled 74, of which 20 were rebuilt from Urie's original locomotives with 54 of the improved design being built new between 1925 and 1927 by Eastleigh Works and the North British Locomotive Co.

As progress on Southern main-line electrification proceeded, the 'King Arthur' class saw its duties altered, being transferred away from the Central Division in 1933, for example, although all passed to BR at Nationalisation. It was the arrival of the Bulleid Pacific designs that led to the first withdrawals in 1953, and all had been withdrawn by the end of 1962. One example, No 777 *Sir Lamiel*, survives in preservation as part of the National Collection. Originally numbered E777 (until the prefix was dropped) and built in June 1925, the locomotive was one of those supplied by North British that acquired the nickname of 'Scotch Arthurs'. The locomotive was withdrawn in October 1961 and is recorded here on the 7th of that month. *Rodney Lissenden*

Southern Railway No 850 *Lord Nelson*

The 16-strong 'Lord Nelson' class of 4-6-0s was designed by Maunsell within strict weight restrictions while seeking to obtain the maximum power possible in order to haul 500-ton trains at an average speed of 55mph. The first of the class — No 850 *Lord Nelson* — was completed at Eastleigh Works in 1926 with the remainder of the class following in 1928/29 following trials with the first engine. At the time of their construction, the class was the most powerful passenger locomotive in service in Britain, a status they held until the completion of the GWR's 'King' class. Designed to haul the SR's heaviest and fastest trains, the locomotives saw duty on, for example, boat train services to the Channel ports but were to be concentrated latterly at Eastleigh where they worked predominantly on services from Waterloo to Southampton and Bournemouth. All 16 of the class were withdrawn in 1961 and 1962, with No 850 entering preservation. The locomotive is seen here at its home shed, Eastleigh, on 10 June 1962 shortly before its withdrawal. *Gavin Morrison*

Great Western Railway No 6000 *King George V*

At the time of their construction, the 'Castle' class 4-6-0s were the heaviest steam locomotives permitted to operate over GWR metals. However, the upgrading of certain sections of the main line during the 1920s permitted Collett to design the ultimate in the long line of GWR 4-6-0s — the 'King' class. Taking full advantage of the increased maximum axle loading, Collett increased the length of the locomotive and its wheelbase in order to accommodate the new standard No 12 boiler. In so doing, he produced the largest, heaviest and most powerful 4-6-0 designed for use on a railway in Britain. In terms of tractive effort, the new class could achieve 40,300lb — a 27%

increase over that produced by the 'Castle' class — but at a cost: the new class was heavily route limited as a result of its weight.

The first of the class, No 6000 *King George V*, emerged from Swindon Works in June 1927 and, when only two months old, was shipped to the USA to take part in the centenary exhibition of the Baltimore & Ohio Railroad. As a result of its trip across the Atlantic, the locomotive was fitted with an American warning bell that it carried thereafter. In total, 30 members of the class were constructed between 1927 and 1930 although one, No 6007 *King William III*, was effectively rebuilt in 1936 following serious accident damage at Shrivenham. The class

dominated the GWR's express services until the late 1950s when the arrival of the diesel-hydraulic types foreshadowed their demise. The whole class was withdrawn in 1962 with No 6000 then entering the National Collection; two other representatives of the type — Nos 6023 *King Edward II* and 6024 *King Edward I* — have also survived, both being restored after having spent some years at the famous scrapyard owned by Woodham Bros at Barry. With its warning bell clearly visible on the front bufferbeam, No 6000 is pictured here while travelling at speed near Widney Manor in 1960. *M. Mensing*

London, Midland & Scottish Railway No 2700
At the Grouping in 1923, George Hughes, from the Lancashire & Yorkshire Railway, was appointed the first Chief Mechanical Engineer of the new LMSR. Although only in his position for a short period — he resigned in 1925 following disagreements with Sir Henry Fowler, latterly CME of the Midland Railway, and with Ernest Trench, the LMS's Chief Civil Engineer — he designed the first of the LMS's 2-6-0 locomotives. The first of these — No 13000 — emerged from Horwich Works in 1926 under the auspices of Fowler, by now appointed as Hughes's successor, and by December 1932 when production

ceased, a total of 245 locomotives had been built. In 1933, Stanier introduced a modified design of Mogul with a further 40 being completed. The original locomotives, initially numbered 13000-13244, were renumbered 2700-2944 in 1934 and thus became Nos 42700-42944 at Nationalisation.

The locomotives, with their high running boards, were atypical of contemporary locomotive design — although it was a feature to become more common later on — and the steeply-angled cylinders were set at a high level in order to keep within the loading gauge of the Midland section. The height of the cylinders earned the locomotives the nickname

initially of 'Spiders' but they soon became better known as 'Crabs'. The class remained intact until 1962 when the first withdrawals occurred. All were withdrawn by the end of January 1967 and No 2700, withdrawn in March 1966, was acquired for the National Collection. Two other examples of the Hughes/Fowler design also survive in preservation, both having been rescued from the Barry scrapyard of Woodham Bros. Here No 42700 awaits its next duty at Llandudno Junction shed in this view taken on 22 June 1963. *Gavin Morrison*

Southern Railway No 925 *Cheltenham*

With the successful introduction of the 'King Arthur' and 'Lord Nelson' classes, the SR's Traffic Manager sought an equivalent type of locomotive capable of handling 400-ton trains at an average speed of 55mph on secondary duties. Maunsell initially proposed the construction of a further class of 4-6-0, but loading gauge restrictions on the line from Tonbridge to Hastings and the ex-SECR route to Ramsgate meant that a 4-4-0 was the result. The first of the 'Schools' class was completed at Eastleigh in

1930, with the remaining 39 examples being constructed there between 1932 and 1935; the locomotives were originally numbered 900-939 (becoming BR Nos 30900-30939). This was the last type of 4-4-0 constructed for use on a railway in Britain and, although regarded as an obsolete wheel arrangement by the date of their introduction, the type proved to be highly successful and represented the most powerful type of this wheel arrangement used on any European railway. Initially based on the SR's South Eastern section, the process of electrification

by BR eventually saw the type transferred to operate elsewhere on the Southern Region. Withdrawals commenced in 1961 with the final examples being condemned the following year. Apart from No 925 in the National Collection, two others of the class survive: No 30926 *Repton,* now repatriated after a period of preservation in North America, and No 928 *Stowe.* Here, No 30925 is pictured at York station on 13 May 1962 some seven months before final withdrawal. *Gavin Morrison*

London, Midland & Scottish Railway No 2500
One of William Stanier's predecessors as CME of the LMS, Sir Henry Fowler, had brought the 2-6-4T wheel arrangement to the railway with the introduction of his 1927 design and, following his appointment, Stanier was authorised to construct further examples of the two-cylinder version of the Fowler design. In fact, however, he took the opportunity to design a brand-new class of 2-6-4T with tapered boiler. Although five were ordered initially, a further 32 were subsequently authorised in order to fulfil a need for improved motive power on the ex-London, Tilbury & Southend Railway lines. The first of the class, No 2500, was built at Derby and delivered in February 1934. This class of locomotive differed from those delivered earlier as they were fitted with three cylinders and Walschaerts valve gear. The class was to operate primarily on the lines out of Fenchurch Street station for their entire career, surviving until the route was electrified. The first of the class was withdrawn in 1960 with all 37 having succumbed by the end of 1962. The pioneering locomotive, renumbered 42500 at Nationalisation, was withdrawn in June 1962 and preserved as part of the National Collection and is the only example of the class to survive. The locomotive has been on loan to the Bressingham Steam Museum for many years and is seen there in steam on 14 July 1983. *Colour-Rail*

London, Midland & Scottish Railway No 5000

In 1932, William Stanier was appointed CME of the LMS and, on his arrival, was faced by an urgent need to improve dramatically the locomotive stock that the company operated. From its pre-Grouping antecedents, the LMS had inherited a considerable variety of locomotives in 1923 and, between then, and Stanier's appointment, his predecessors in the role of CME had not addressed the need for locomotives capable of dealing with the increasing weight and speed demanded at the time. A Swindon man, Stanier was fully aware of the benefits of standardisation and, during his years with the LMS, he designed a number of highly successful classes

that revolutionised the LMS's operations. Aware of the need to produce a mixed-traffic locomotive capable of handling a wide range of services over the LMS network, Stanier came up with the 'Black 5' class 4-6-0s, of which the first, No 5000, emerged from Crewe Works in February 1935. In all, a total of 842 of the class were constructed between then and 1951, making it second only to the '8F' class 2-8-0 in terms of numbers built amongst Stanier's various designs.

Although the basic design was modified over a period of time, based on operational experience, the 'Black 5s' represented a hugely successful type and saw service over much of the LMS network operating

both passenger and freight trains. The first of the type was withdrawn in 1961 but a number remained in service right through to the end of main-line steam in August 1968. Indeed, it was a pair of 'Black 5s' that double-headed the official last BR steam special on 11 August 1968. The original locomotive, by now renumbered 45000, was withdrawn in October 1967 and was preserved as part of the National Collection. Apart from this example, no fewer than 16 other examples of the type have survived into preservation. The locomotive is recorded here at Blackpool North on 21 September 1967, shortly before its withdrawal.
P. J. Fitton/Colour-Rail

London & North Eastern Railway
No 4771 *Green Arrow*

By the early 1930s, the growth of road haulage was starting to have a dramatic impact on the railways and, in order to counter the competition, the railways sought to innovate. Among the schemes adopted by the LNER was an express parcels service called 'Green Arrow'. To power these trains, a new class of locomotive was required and, following examination of a number of alternative designs, Sir Nigel Gresley determined upon the 'V2' class 2-6-2. The first of the

class, No 4771 to be named, appropriately, *Green Arrow*, emerged from Doncaster Works in June 1936. The class was the first three-cylinder 2-6-2 design to be produced in Britain. Initially, five of the type were constructed, designed for both express passenger and parcels traffic, but ultimately 184 of the class were built between 1936 and 1944, with both Darlington and Doncaster handling the work.

Following the LNER's second renumbering scheme of 1946, the class became Nos 800-983 and thus 60800-60983 after Nationalisation. The first of

the class was withdrawn in 1962 and all had succumbed by 1966. The pioneer locomotive, now numbered 60800, was withdrawn in August 1962. Since preservation and the reappearance of main-line steam on BR, the locomotive, restored as LNER No 4771, was a regular performer on both the main line and preserved railways until final withdrawal in 2008. The locomotive is pictured here at Doncaster on 12 April 1959. *John Edgington*

Southern Railway No 2090 (EMU)

In 1912 the London & South Western Railway announced a programme of converting some 92 route miles to third-rail dc electric traction. These first routes were largely those that it operated in the suburbs of London, but it started a process by which much of the future BR Southern Region was to be electrified. Following the Grouping in 1923, the Southern Railway continued to extend the third-rail network, with the lines covered extending beyond those of the suburbs and, between 1935 and 1938, the longer distance lines from London to Eastbourne, Alton, Portsmouth and Reading, along with the line from Portsmouth to Bognor Regis were all converted.

In order to operate services over these newly-electrified lines, the SR constructed the '2-BIL' class EMUs. These two-car sets, constructed at Eastleigh on frames supplied from Lancing, were so-called as they had two toilets ('bi-lavatory'), one in each of the coaches. In all, 152 of the class were built between 1935 and 1938. Under the TOPS scheme the units became Class 401 but all were withdrawn by the early 1970s. Only one of the two-car sets — formed of 1937-built Nos S10656S (Driver Motor Brake Third) and S12123S (Driving Trailer Composite) — survives in preservation as part of the National Collection. It has been used for special services in preservation in restored SR green livery and, on 22 November 1986, is recorded at Waterloo station.
Harry Luff/Online Transport Archive

London & North Eastern Railway No 4468 *Mallard*

During the early 1930s Nigel Gresley and his personal assistant Oliver Bulleid were fully conversant with technical and stylistic developments in Europe — indeed, Bulleid had worked in France during the early part of is career and Gresley visited the country in 1933. Among the innovations that appeared during these years was the German streamlined 'Flying Hamburger' diesel unit. The LNER seriously investigated the possibility of constructing a similar unit under licence for the East Coast main line, but decided against it, preferring to see the further development of steam traction. The result was the 'A4' class of Pacific locomotive, the first of which — No 2509 *Silver Link* — was unveiled in September 1935. Built by Doncaster Works, the development of the new class had been

rapid, with design work only starting in March of that year. The success of the first quartet led to further orders, with an eventual total of 35 being constructed between 1935 and 1938. Of these, four were delivered with Kylchap double exhausts and a large double chimney. These proved to be the most successful although it was not until after World War 2 that the remainder of the class were converted to double-chimney format.

One of these double-chimney locomotives, No 4468 *Mallard,* was to achieve fame when, on 3 July 1938, the locomotive achieved a world speed record — which still stands — for a steam locomotive, of 126mph. After the war, the locomotives underwent some modification; in particular, the valencing around the valve gear was removed. The class was to remain associated with East Coast main line

expresses until the introduction of the 'Deltic' class diesel-electrics in 1961, but a number were to have an Indian summer, thereafter operating expresses between Aberdeen and Glasgow. Of the 35 built, 34 passed to BR in 1948 — the exception was one destroyed in a German air raid on York on 29 April 1942. They were all withdrawn between 1962 and 1966. On withdrawal in April 1963 *Mallard* — by now renumbered 60022 — was claimed for the National Collection, with a further five examples surviving in private preservation (two of which are in North America). On 19 August 1961, the locomotive is pictured at Stoke Tunnel, close to the scene of its record-breaking run, with the 2.45pm service from King's Cross to Newcastle. *Hugh Ballantyne*

London, Midland & Scottish Railway No 6229
Duchess of Hamilton

Although William Stanier had designed an earlier class of Pacific locomotive — the 'Princess Royal', of which two survive in preservation — he was aware both that the fastest West Coast expresses needed improved performance and that the LNER had already developed its streamlined 'A4' class. In an era when there was considerable competition between the East Coast and West Coast routes as well as with the growing road and aviation industries, Stanier needed to come up with a new design that could capture the public imagination. In the 'Princess Coronation' or 'Duchess' class he produced a design that fulfilled these expectations, particularly as the first locomotives emerged from Crewe Works in a bright blue livery. Initially, five locomotives, Nos 6220–6224, were ordered, but further examples — in both streamlined and non-streamlined form — soon followed. In 1939, for the New York World's Fair, the newly-completed streamlined No 6229 was shipped across the Atlantic for display, albeit in the guise of No 6220 *Coronation*. While in the USA, the locomotive was fitted with a headlight and bell and, as a result of the outbreak of World War 2, it remained over there for four years.

A total of 20 locomotives had been constructed by the end of 1939; between then and 1948, when production ceased, a further 18 were completed. Of the total built, 24 were built in streamlined form and, after the war, experience with maintenance of these examples led to a decision to remove the streamlined casing. All had been converted to non-streamline form by early 1949. Initially, it was possible to identify those so treated by a tapered top to the smokebox, although this feature was eventually eliminated. The class continued to dominate West Coast main line expresses until the early 1960s, but all 38 were withdrawn between 1962 and 1964 with two other examples — apart from BR No 46229 in the National Collection — surviving in preservation. Although No 46229 was originally preserved in its non-streamlined form, the National Railway Museum is currently undertaking a project to restore the locomotive to its original appearance. Here, the locomotive can be seen approaching Glasgow Central with a down West Coast main line express in its final, non-streamlined, condition. *Derek Penney*

Southern Railway No C1 (33001)

During the course of World War 2 it became apparent to the SR that it needed additional freight locomotives to cope with the excess traffic which the war was bringing to a railway that was predominantly passenger-orientated. In theory, Oliver Bulleid could have perpetuated an earlier design, Mansell's 'Q' class of 1938, but, given the exigencies of the time, he opted for a brand-new and radical design — the 'Q1' class 0-6-0. The first of these, numbered C1, was completed in March 1942 and the entire class of 40, all built at Brighton, was delivered by the end of the year.

The design owed much to the need to save precious raw materials and also to minimise weight so that they would be able to operate over the majority of the SR's network. The patented Bulleid-Firth-Brown wheels were, for example, 10% lighter than conventional spoked driving wheels and each locomotive weighed some 14 tons less than a similar engine of conventional design. With a tractive effort of 30,000lb, the locomotives were also significantly more powerful than the earlier 'Q' class 0-6-0. Although the design was not perpetuated postwar, the 'Q1' proved itself a successful design and, allocated over much of the Southern area, continued in service until withdrawn between 1963 and 1966. Only one member of the class, the original No C1 (renumbered 33001 by BR in 1948), has survived and became part of the National Collection on withdrawal. It is pictured here in service on the Bluebell Railway, its home for a number of years. *Bruce Oliver*

Southern Railway No 21C151 / 34051
Winston Churchill

Following on from Bulleid's first design of Pacific locomotive for the Southern Railway (see 65), a second design emerged in 1945. This was outwardly very similar to the 'Merchant Navy' class but was lighter and intended for use over those routes barred to the earlier type as a result of their weight. The first of the class emerged from Brighton Works in June 1945 and, destined for operation primarily on the lines from Waterloo to Exeter and beyond, the locomotives became known as the 'West Country' class with names associated with that area. A total of

110 of the Bulleid Light Pacifics were constructed, split between the 'West Country' class with 66 examples and the 'Battle of Britain' class with 44. Apart from the altered bias in terms of naming, there were no other differences between the two types. The locomotives were built at either Eastleigh or Brighton between 1945 and 1951.

As with the 'Merchant Navy' class, experience in operation showed that there were weaknesses with Bulleid's design and a total of 60 were rebuilt between June 1957 and April 1961. In January 1965, Sir Winston Churchill, Britain's wartime Prime Minister died, and, following a state funeral on

30 January, his coffin was carried by a special train from Waterloo to Handborough (north of Oxford). This was hauled, appropriately, by 'Battle of Britain' class No 34051 *Winston Churchill* and, following withdrawal, it was selected to form part of the National Collection. Of the 110 locomotives built, 20 survive in preservation, and of these, half are in original 'unrebuilt' condition, including No 34051 — built at Brighton in December 1946 — which is recorded here on 4 April 1965 departing from Bournemouth West with an LCGB special to London Waterloo. *Hugh Ballantyne*

Great Western Railway No 9400

The GWR's preferred version of the standard 0-6-0T was the pannier tank and a large number of this type of locomotive, in various classes, were built. The last of the type to be designed and built by the GWR before the Nationalisation of the railways in 1948 was the '9400' class designed by F. W. Hawksworth, Collett's successor as the GWR's CME. The first 10 were built in 1947 and were the last locomotives to be completed by the GWR prior to 1 January 1948.

The class resulted from a requirement for additional 0-6-0PTs and, rather than perpetuate the earlier '5700' design, Hawksworth was instructed to produce a modernised version. This he achieved through using a standard No 10 tapered boiler and drumhead smokebox. However, the result of these modifications was a locomotive that, overall, was less successful than its predecessors. In particular, its overall weight was slightly greater, which reduced its route availability, and the cab was less conveniently configured for the driver.

Despite these drawbacks, no fewer than 210 locomotives of the class were constructed between 1947 and 1956; unusually for a GWR design, all bar the first 10 were manufactured by outside contractors. The first 10 were fitted with superheaters and originally delivered in GWR plain green livery. Withdrawals of the class started in March 1959 with the National Collection's example, No 9400, succumbing in December of the same year. The last examples were withdrawn in 1965 and one other class member, No 9466, also survives in preservation. No 9400 is pictured in Swindon Works on 1 April 1962. *Colour Rail*

British Railway No 35029 *Ellerman Lines*

One of the most controversial of British locomotive engineers, Oliver Bulleid was appointed CME of the Southern Railway in 1937 having spent the bulk of his career prior to that date with the LNER and its predecessor, the Great Northern. The first of the CME's new designs appeared in 1941 although the construction of a batch of 10 locomotives had been authorised prior to the outbreak of World War 2, in 1938. Set the task of producing a locomotive capable of 60mph on services to the Channel ports and 70mph on the ex-LSWR main line, Bulleid eventually settled on the 4-6-2 wheel arrangement. However, as delivered in 1941, the first of the 'Merchant Navy' class represented a radical departure from the designs of earlier Pacific type locomotives.

Despite the wartime environment in which the class was launched, the new locomotives — described as 'air-smoothed' when first completed — included a host of new features including a patented design of driving wheel and a welded steel firebox. A total of 30 of the class were constructed at Eastleigh between 1941 and 1949 although experience in operation proved the locomotives expensive and prone to wheel slipping. As a result, all were completely rebuilt between February 1956 and October 1959. As rebuilt, the locomotives proved much more reliable in service although these improvements came too late to extend the locomotives' lives significantly as, by the late 1950s, the process of dieselisation and electrification was to lead to steam's rapid elimination. The first of the class was withdrawn in 1964 with the last succumbing three years later. Although no example was initially selected for the National Collection, No 35029 was acquired from the famous Barry scrapyard for conversion into a static exhibit suitably sectioned to show how a steam locomotive works. Apart from No 35029 — pictured here at Nine Elms shed in 'air-smoothed' condition on 14 October 1952, when only just over three years old — nine other examples of the type have survived into preservation.
John Edgington

British Railways No 26020

Although the LNER had planned for the conversion of the ex-Great Central main line from Sheffield to Manchester via Woodhead to 1,500V dc before 1939, the onset of World War 2 inevitably delayed the project. After the war, work was resumed but it was not until 1954 that the electrification scheme was completed with the opening of the new Woodhead Tunnel. In order to provide motive power for the route, two classes of locomotive were ordered: 57 Bo-Bos, later designated Class 76, for use primarily on the freight traffic that was the raison d'être of the scheme, and six Co-Cos, later designated Class 77, for use on passenger services. The former were

based on an example constructed by the LNER, No 6701, which had been built in 1941 and, following a period on loan to the Dutch Railways from 1947 to 1952, had been named *Tommy*. The new Bo-Bo locomotives, Nos 260012-57, were constructed by Doncaster and Gorton works. Passenger services over the Woodhead route ceased in January 1970 but, by that date, the Class 77s had been withdrawn and transferred to the Netherlands. (Subsequent to withdrawal there, two examples have returned to the UK for preservation.)

The Woodhead route was used primarily for coal traffic, with the Class 76s usually operating in multiple on trains from the Yorkshire coalfield.

However, despite the usefulness of the route as a diversionary line for passenger traffic, a perceived need to rationalise the number of lines across the Pennines resulted in the closure of the Woodhead route in July 1981. Unfortunately, the original locomotive, had not been preserved on withdrawal in 1970, but one of the production examples, No 26020, (as No 7602a) , was secured for the National Collection. Here, an interesting line-up at Doncaster Works on 10 September 1977 sees the Class 76 awaiting restoration in the company of a Class 55 'Deltic' and a Class 50 — types not normally seen alongside the 1,500V locomotives.
Colin J. Marsden

British Railways No 70013 *Oliver Cromwell*

Following the Nationalisation of the railway industry in 1948, the newly-created British Railways initially perpetuated the locomotive designs inherited from the earlier 'Big Four' companies. However, in January 1951, the first of the new BR Standard types emerged from Crewe Works. This was No 70000, a Pacific built to the design of the BR's Chief Mechanical Engineer, Robert A. Riddles. Named *Britannia*, the locomotive was to be the first of 999 Standards built between then and 1960. Following on from No 70000, a further 54 examples of the 'Britannia' class Pacifics were constructed between January 1951 and September 1954. The locomotives were initially allocated to the Eastern, Southern — where No 70004 *William Shakespeare* was put on display as part of the Festival of Britain display — and Western regions, where they were to prove a considerable success. Later examples were allocated to the Scottish and London Midland regions and, as steam was gradually replaced elsewhere, the class was gradually concentrated on to the LMR.

Withdrawals began in 1965 and, by the end of 1967, only one example, No 70013 *Oliver Cromwell*, remained in service. This locomotive, rather than the class pioneer No 70000 (which had suffered accident damage), was ultimately selected to join the National Collection and, following withdrawal in August 1968, travelled light engine to Norwich — the last main-line steam locomotive in East Anglia until the boom in steam excursion traffic — prior to being put on display along with other locomotives from the National Collection at the Bressingham Steam Museum of the late Alan Bloom. Although No 70000 was not selected for preservation as part of the National Collection, it was ultimately preserved privately and at the time of writing was under restoration for further operation on the main line. No 70013 was extracted from Bressingham and, following a thorough restoration at Loughborough, returned to the main line in 2008. In this view of Southport Chapel Street station, No 70013 is seen having arrived at the head of a special shortly before its withdrawal. *J. G. Parkinson/ Online Transport Archive*

British Railways No 13079

The single largest class of diesel motive power built for use on BR is represented in the National Collection by No 13079 (later Nos D3079 and 08064). Based around the earlier LMS/English Electric design introduced in 1944, the future Class 08 first emerged from Derby Works in October 1952. Between then and 1962, when production ceased, no fewer than 1,193 locomotives of a similar design had been constructed. Destined to become BR's standard diesel-electric shunter, the 350hp 0-6-0 was a familiar sight throughout the BR network — indeed, the class remains heavily active on the National Network more than 50 years after it was first introduced, and is the only class of shunting locomotive still operational in significant numbers. Beyond those that remain in service on the main line, a number have also found subsequent careers in industry and in preservation. The locomotive, restored to original BR black livery, is seen at York on 23 May 1995. *Colin J. Marsden*

English Electric *Deltic*

Both before and after the 1955 Modernisation Plan, a number of prototype and experimental locomotives were operated on British Railways. Of these the most distinctive — perhaps as a result of its bright blue livery — was the English Electric-built prototype Co-Co *Deltic*. At the time of its construction in 1955, English Electric had hopes for a significant export market for the design — hence the centre headlight — but these expectations were ill-founded. The locomotive's name derived from the use of two 'Deltic' diesel engines manufactured by D. Napier & Son, a company that normally specialised in the construction of engines for the marine industry. Largely built at English Electric's Dick Kerr Works in Preston, the locomotive first entered service based in Liverpool in December 1955.

It remained on the London Midland Region until transferred to the Eastern Region in 1959 where it began trials on East Coast main line services. Proving successful in operation, albeit not without incident, the locomotive paved the way for the construction of the 22-strong Class 55 (see p75), introduced in 1961. However, in March that year, contemporaneously with the delivery of the first production locomotives, *Deltic* suffered an engine failure and was taken out of service. In 1963 the locomotive was restored externally and presented to the Science Museum for display. It arrived in London on 28 April 1963 and was destined to remain part of the Science Museum display until relocated to the National Railway Museum in October 1993. On 23 July 1960, *Deltic* was recorded at Doncaster station. *Bruce Nathan/Colour-Rail*

British Railways No D8000

In 1955, the British Transport Commission launched its Modernisation Plan with the intention of replacing the railway's entire steam locomotive fleet over a period of years with a combination of diesel and electric traction. However, before committing the significant investment involved in the dieselisation programme, trial batches of a number of locomotive types were acquired in the various power ranges: the Pilot Scheme locomotives. Type 1 locomotives were those destined to have a power range of between 800hp and 1,000hp and a number of manufacturers were commissioned to produce locomotives of this power. This included English Electric, from which a batch of 20 locomotives was ordered. The first of these, No D8000, was delivered in June 1957 and

was thus the first Modernisation Plan locomotive to be delivered. The future Class 20s proved themselves to be the most successful of the Type 1 diesel-electric locomotives and a total of 228 examples were built between then and February 1968 by Vulcan Foundry at Newton-le-Willows and by Robert Stephenson & Hawthorns at Darlington.

The Pilot Scheme locomotives were initially allocated to the London Midland Region for use on both passenger and freight traffic, but the class was also to see service widely on the Eastern and Scottish regions. Largely used on freight traffic, where they regularly operated in multiple on coal traffic, the class was also used on passenger services, particularly in the summer when their lack of train heating equipment was not a disadvantage.

The first withdrawals occurred in the mid-1970s, but did not begin on a large scale until the 1980s. With the arrival of newer and more powerful locomotives, the class's days were numbered although a handful remain operational on the main line some 50 years after their first introduction. Withdrawn in December 1980, the pioneering No D8000, which had been renumbered 20050 under the TOPS scheme in February 1974, was claimed for the National Collection. Apart from No D8000 a number of other examples have also been preserved.

Here, the locomotive is recorded in 1985 following repainting into its original all-over green livery with no yellow end warning panels, for display within the museum at York. *David Ware*

British Railways No D5500

Following on from the delivery of the first Type 1 diesel-electric locomotive, the first of the Type 2 power range — covering locomotives rated at 1,000-1,365hp — was delivered from Brush in October 1957. As with the Class 20, an initial batch of 20 locomotives had been ordered. These were delivered to the Eastern Region, where they were based for their entire working lives, and, following a successful introduction, a large-scale order was placed, although the main production batch of locomotives was fitted with electro-pneumatic control equipment as opposed to the electro-magnetic type installed in the Pilot Scheme batch. Ultimately, 263 examples of the class were constructed before production ceased in 1962.

The original locomotives were rated at 1,250hp but the production batch was rerated to 1,365hp. In 1964, following problems with fatigue in the type's original Mirrlees engines, replacement English Electric engines rated at 1,470hp were installed in the entire class over a period of years.

The bulk of the class was based on the Eastern Region for most of its career, but the type was also used by the Western Region. Under the TOPS scheme, those not re-engined were designated Class 30, although none ever carried a 30xxx number as the programme for engine replacement was completed before the renumbering was commenced. Therefore, all became Class 31. The non-standard Pilot Scheme locomotives, Nos D5500-D5519, were

classified as 31/0 (with the exception of No D5518 which became Class 31/1 No 31101) and were destined to be early casualties, being withdrawn between 1976 and 1980. On withdrawal in July 1976 No D5500 passed to the National Collection. As with the Class 20s, large-scale withdrawals of the Class 31s commenced in the late 1980s as newer classes of locomotive were introduced. Again, a small number remain operational on the main line today. Apart from No D5500 a number of other examples have also been preserved. Pictured at Doncaster Works on 10 September 1977, No D5500 was restored to original green livery without yellow end warning panels prior to display at the museum.

Colin J. Marsden

British Railways No E5001

At Nationalisation in 1948, BR inherited three electric locomotives from the Southern Railway. These were fitted for operation both on third-rail and, in yards where the presence of a third rail could cause danger, overhead catenary. Based on the experience gained with these locomotives, 24 new locomotives were ordered in 1955 for use as part of Kent Coast electrification scheme. The first of the locomotives, No E5000, was delivered from Doncaster Works in December 1958 with the final example appearing in November 1960; all were allocated from new to the South Eastern Division. Designed for use on passenger services, such as the 'Golden Arrow' and 'Night Ferry', and on freight, by the mid-1960s traffic patterns were changing and there was a reduced requirement for the class. As a result, 10 locomotives (including No E5000) were rebuilt as electro-diesels for use on the South Western Division. The other 14 members of the class, by now designated Class 71, remained in service until all were placed in store in late 1976 with their work transferred to either Class 33 or Class 73 haulage. Withdrawal *en masse* followed in November 1977 with No E5001 passing to the National Collection. In 1992, No E5001 was restored for use on the main line and was used on specials for a number of years thereafter. No E5001 is pictured passing Longhedge Junction with an excursion from Luton to Margate on 26 July 1959. *R. C. Riley*

British Railways No 51192 (DMU)

From the early 1950s onwards BR introduced significant numbers of diesel multiple-units to replace steam-operated passenger trains on suburban and lightly-trafficked lines. These new units were to prove popular with passengers and economic in use, undoubtedly helping a significant number of lines to survive longer than they would have done without this investment. Production of the first-generation DMUs by both BR and outside contractors had largely ceased by the early 1960s, but many were to see service through to the late 1980s and early 1990s. Among the most successful of the first-generation designs was the Class 101 produced by Metro-Cammell in Birmingham between 1956 and 1959. The last of the type were not to be withdrawn until December 2003 by which date some were more than 47 years old.

Within the National Collection is DMBS (Driving Motor Brake Second) No 51192, which, together with driving trailer (DTCL) No 54352, is currently based on the East Lancashire Railway and restored to green livery. A number of Class 101 units survive in preservation and the National Collection also includes a Class 108 two-car set (Nos 51562 and 51922), which dates from 1959. *Bruce Oliver*

British Railways No D200

The third example of a class drawn from those delivered as Pilot Scheme locomotives under the Modernisation Plan of 1955 is Class 40, represented in the National Collection by No D200. Type 4 covered locomotives rated between 2,000hp and 2,750hp, with 10 being ordered from English Electric rated at 2,000hp. Produced at Vulcan Foundry, the first of the class was completed in March 1958 and was allocated to the Eastern Region. This locomotive first operated in service on 18 March 1958 when it hauled a special from London Liverpool Street to Norwich. The remaining nine locomotives of the initial batch were also allocated to the Eastern Region. Further orders, for another 190 were issued, with production being divided between EE's Vulcan Foundry and Robert Stephenson & Hawthorns, with the final example entering service in September 1962.

Nicknamed 'Whistlers' by enthusiasts, as a result of their distinctive sound, the class was allocated from new to the Eastern, North Eastern, London Midland, and Scottish regions, seeing service on both passenger and freight duties. Withdrawal of the class in significant numbers began in the mid-1970s and all had been withdrawn by the end of January 1985 with the exception of No D200 — by this date renumbered 40122 under the TOPS scheme — which was retained by BR for the operation of specials. On final withdrawal in May 1988, the locomotive passed to the National Collection. Apart from No D200, six other Class 40s survive in preservation. In this view, taken at Agecroft on 24 July 1985, No D200, by this date the solitary survivor of the class on the main line, is seen hauling one of the specials for which the locomotive had been retained. *Gavin Morrison*

British Railways No 03090

During the early 1950s BR acquired a large number of small shunting locomotives from a variety of manufacturers and, based upon the best features of these earlier models, decided to construct a standard class of medium-wheelbase 0-6-0 diesel-mechanical shunters. Ordered in 1955, the first of the type were delivered in 1957 and by the time construction ceased in 1962 a total of 230 had been built by both Swindon and Doncaster works. However, by the mid-1960s, much of the traffic for which the type had been designed, primarily the shunting of traditional goods yards, was disappearing as the railway network shrank and a large proportion of the wagon-load freight was lost to the road haulage industry. As a result, withdrawals of the class commenced towards the end of that decade although a large number were to find subsequent careers in industry. Those that survived with BR were eventually to be classified '03' under the TOPS scheme and renumbered accordingly. With a handful of exceptions, all were withdrawn by British Rail by 1990; such was the type's usefulness, however, that a large number have survived into preservation alongside No 03090, which became part of the National Collection when withdrawn from York depot in July 1976. Three years after withdrawal, No 03090 is seen on display within the museum. *Colin J. Marsden*

British Railways No D2860

Although by the late 1950s, BR had developed its own design of small diesel shunter, there remained a need for a very short wheelbase locomotive. The result was a batch of 20 0-4-0s constructed by the Yorkshire Engine Co. Delivered between September 1960 and December 1961, the locomotives had a wheelbase of only 6ft 0in and were fitted with hydraulic transmission. The class proved highly successful for the types of traffic for which they were designed, such as shunting the docks in Liverpool, but as with other types of shunter, the traffic for which they were designed was gradually disappearing, with the result that withdrawals commenced in 1969.

Classified '02' under the TOPS scheme, only three examples survived to carry their new numbers and all had been withdrawn by 1975. However, No D2860, withdrawn in December 1970, was placed in long-term store with the intention, ultimately, of it being preserved. After almost a decade out of use, the locomotive was refurbished by Thomas Hill and transferred to the National Railway Museum in 1978. At the museum, the locomotive is both an exhibit, portraying a small diesel shunter, and a useful working locomotive in that its short wheelbase is ideal for the movement of other museum exhibits. On 21 April 1993, No D2860 positions 'V2' No 4771 and Class 40 No D200 in front of the by-now long-closed diesel depot at York. The demolition of this building facilitated the considerable expansion of the museum's display space. *Colin J. Marsden*

British Railways No 84001

As with the introduction of BR's diesel fleet in the late 1950s, the development of the 25kV ac electrics for use on the planned electrification of the West Coast main line saw production split between a number of manufacturers, including Beyer Peacock and English Electric. The 'AL4' class — later designated Class 84 under the TOPS scheme — was contracted to the North British Locomotive Co Ltd of Glasgow with production commencing in 1959. By that time, the once important company was in terminal decline and, just as its main-line diesel locomotives produced for BR proved disappointing, the 10 locomotives of Class 84 were also troublesome in service. Delivered between March 1961 and March the following year, and based at Manchester Longsight, the locomotives — numbered originally E3036-E3045 — were soon experiencing failures with the result that, in April 1963, the entire class was temporarily withdrawn for repair work. Although this alleviated some of the problems, the class remained vulnerable, again being temporarily withdrawn in 1967.

By the mid-1970s, as a small and unreliable type, the Class 84s were destined for early withdrawal, with the entire class being taken out of traffic between April 1977 and November 1980. Withdrawn in January 1979, No 84001 was initially loaned by BR to the National Railway Museum for display in connection with an exhibition on electric traction. It was originally intended that the locomotive would form part of the National Collection only until an example of either Class 86 or 87 was added. In the event, however, No 84001 has been retained and is in the care of the AC Locomotive Group at Barrow Hill, despite the addition recently of No 87001 to the National Collection. Here, No 84001 is pictured in the main museum at York in 1979 shortly after its arrival. *S. J. Boon*

British Railways No D6700

The most numerous of BR's Type 3 diesel-electrics, with a total of 309 locomotives built by English Electric and Robert Stephenson & Hawthorns between November 1960 and November 1965, was Class 37. The initial batch of 30 locomotives was allocated to Stratford depot for use on the Eastern Region, with later examples allocated to the North Eastern, Eastern and Western regions. Designed for use on both passenger and freight traffic, the class was successful once an initial tendency to suffer bogie fractures was solved. Over the years, the class's area of operation expanded to include Scotland, where they replaced earlier diesel-electrics on services through the Highlands. From the mid-1980s onwards, a number of the class were refurbished thereby extending their lives and the vast majority survived into the 1990s; it was only Privatisation and the massive investment in new, more powerful Class 66 and 67 designs that led to the rapid withdrawal of the type although, more than 40 years since the last of the type was built, a significant number of the class remain in front-line service with others now having entered preservation. The National Collection was presented by EWS with the first example built, No D6700 (or No 37119 and later 37350, as it became under the TOPS scheme) in 2000, in full working order and it has never officially been withdrawn. It is recorded here in Rail Blue as No D6700 on a northbound goods at Croxdale on 14 April 1972. *Derek Cross*

British Railways No D9002
King's Own Yorkshire Light Infantry

As a result of its success with the twin-engined 'Deltic' prototype, the British Transport Commission ordered a production batch of 22 locomotives from English Electric in March 1958. With the construction work handled at Vulcan Foundry, Newton-le-Willows, the first two of the locomotives, Nos D9000 and D9001, emerged in January 1961. The entire batch was delivered by mid-1962 and, primarily intended to replace the 'A4' class Pacifics on East Coast main line duties, the 22 locomotives were allocated to depots on the Scottish, North Eastern and Eastern

regions. Fitted with twin Napier 'Deltic' engines, the locomotives were rated at 3,300hp and were thus the most powerful of BR's first-generation of diesel-electric locomotive.

They were named soon after introduction; those on the ScR and ER after British Army regiments, while those allocated to the NER received the names of well-known racehorses. Highly successful, the class dominated services over the East Coast main line from London to Yorkshire, the northeast and Scotland until the introduction of the InterCity 125s in the late 1970s. Following the arrival of these units, the 'Deltics' found additional duties operating on

services from Liverpool to Newcastle. However, the first two examples were withdrawn in early 1980 with the final members of the class succumbing in January 1982. Apart from No D9002 with the National Collection — chosen, according to some, as a result of its abbreviated name 'KOYLI', being a homophone of the museum's then director, the late Dr John Coiley — five other examples of the class currently survive in preservation. Here, No 55002, as the locomotive was renumbered under the TOPS scheme, is seen passing the site of Beeston station, near Leeds, on 5 November 1978. *Gavin Morrison*

British Railways No D1023 *Western Fusilier*

The only example of BR's fleet of diesel-hydraulic locomotives to feature in the National Collection, No D1023 *Western Fusilier* was one of 74 locomotives delivered by Swindon and Crewe works between 1961 and 1964. Rated at 2,700hp, the Class 52 locomotives were the most powerful of the various types of diesel-hydraulic delivered for BR(W) operation. Designed for express passenger services from London Paddington to the West Country or South Wales, the locomotives were highly successful. However, the much reduced need for traction following the radical reduction of the railway network after the publication of Beeching report in the early 1960s allowed BR to rationalise its traction requirements, with the non-standard diesel-hydraulic classes being among the first to succumb. The first threat to the 'Westerns' came with the transfer of the Class 50s to the Western Region following the completion of the scheme to electrify the West Coast main line.

Withdrawals commenced in the spring of 1973 but it was not until February 1977 that the last representative of the class was taken out of service. Among those that survived until the end was No D1023, which was selected to become part of the National Collection. This was not No D1023's first visit to York, as in February 1976 it had brought an excursion to the city. Apart from No D1023, six other members of the class survive in preservation. Although the locomotives were noted during their early career for a variety of liveries — maroon, green and some one-offs such as Desert Sand and Golden Ochre — the class spent the bulk of their life in Rail Blue and it is in this livery that No D1023 is pictured arriving at Paddington on 23 December 1975 at the head of the 15.25 service from Cardiff via Gloucester. *Norman Preedy*

British Railways No 47798 *Prince William*

By the late 1950s, with the process of conversion from steam traction now firmly entrenched, the British Transport Commission sought designs for a new generation of Type 4 locomotives. A number of possible designs were submitted but that produced by Brush was ultimately selected. An initial batch of 20 locomotives was ordered and the first of these, No D1500, was delivered in September 1962. Further batches were ordered and, in total, 512 of the class were built by Brush at Loughborough and by Crewe Works before production ceased in January 1967. Versatile locomotives, members of the class were allocated to each of the BR regions with the exception of the Southern during their long career. Used on both passenger and freight traffic, the Brush Type 4s, designated Class 47 under the TOPS scheme, were the mainstay of the BR diesel locomotive fleet for many years and a limited number remain in operation today with further examples having been modified to form Class 57.

No 47798 was built at Crewe Works and entered service in February 1965 as No D1656 allocated to Landore depot in Cardiff. A Western Region locomotive for most of its BR career, it was renumbered 47072 in January 1974 as part of the TOPS scheme. Undergoing modification, the locomotive was renumbered 47609 in April 1984 and was named *Firefly*; it retained the name when fitted with extended range fuel tanks and renumbered 47834 in July 1989. It was to be renumbered and renamed 47798 *Prince William* on 8 May 1985 for use on Royal Train duties along with No 47799 *Prince Henry*. The locomotive was withdrawn in August 2004 and presented to the National Collection by EWS. Apart from No 47798 a number are also in private preservation. Seen on Royal Train duties on 27 March 1997, No 47998 heads through Bradford Junction, Shipley. *Gavin Morrison*

British Railways No 33116

Although the Southern Region's policy was to replace steam traction largely with third-rail electrification, there was a need for diesel traction for certain services and routes. In analysing these requirements, it was found that a mid-powered Bo-Bo would be suitable and the end result was the Type 3 (later Class 33), rated at 1,550hp, built by the Birmingham Railway Carriage & Wagon Co. Ordered in 1957, the first of the 98-strong fleet was delivered on 4 December 1959. Initially, the entire class, which included 12 narrower bodied locomotives for use of the gauge-restricted line from Tonbridge to Hastings, was allocated to the South Eastern Division but, in 1965, one locomotive was fitted with an experimental push-pull system for use in connection with hauling stock on the line from Waterloo over the non-electrified section from Bournemouth to Weymouth, following the final withdrawal of Southern Region main-line steam in mid-1967. Proving a success, 19 locomotives were thus fitted; these locomotives, reclassified as Class 33/1 under the TOPS scheme, dominated these services until the route through to Weymouth was electrified.

Apart from a few withdrawn prematurely owing to accident damage, withdrawal of the Class 33 fleet commenced in the mid-1980s, although a number remain in operation on the main line in the post-Privatisation era. One of the push-pull fitted locomotives, No 33116 (originally No D6535), was added to the National Collection following withdrawal; a number of other examples can also be found in private preservation. Here, in 1982, No 33116 approaches the terminus at Weymouth hauling two rakes of the non-powered '4TC' stock that the locomotive was converted to work with in push-pull mode. *M. Mensing*

British Rail No APT-E

While elsewhere in the world high-speed railway technology was developing apace by the early 1970s, in Britain the railway industry had a problem: its existing infrastructure was unsuitable for high-speed running, but there was unlikely to be sufficient investment to improve it. Thus the engineers started to look at alternative methods of increasing speed on existing track. One result was the High Speed Train, which was ideal for lines such as the East Coast main line which were reasonably engineered, but less so for the more sinuous West Coast route. In order to maximise the speed over this line, the Railway Technical Centre at Derby developed the concept of the tilting train. This radical approach — which also used hydro-kinetic braking — was first tested in the APT-E, an experimental gas turbine-powered four-car unit introduced in July 1972.

The four-set, comprising two power cars (Nos PC1 and PC2) and two trailer cars (Nos TC1 and TC2), was built at Derby and quickly established a new high-speed record on Britain's railways of 152.3mph while being tested on the Western Region. The unit was withdrawn in June 1976 and claimed for the National Collection. The three prototype units — the ac electric APT-Ps — were publicly launched in December 1981 but proved less than satisfactory in service and were soon withdrawn. Although the class briefly re-entered service in 1984, by this date the likelihood of acquiring the planned fleet of APTs was remote and the type was again withdrawn. The National Collection includes one of the APT-P power cars, No 49006, and a full rake is on display at The Railway Age in Crewe. APT-E is seen here on the Old Dalby test line. *Colin J. Marsden*

British Rail No 41001

By the early 1970s, British Rail had a potentially serious problem: as a result of the Modernisation Plan and the subsequent report on the reshaping of Britain's railways that had effectively reduced significantly BR's traction requirements, the railways faced the likelihood of trying to operate the railways with an increasingly aged and unreliable fleet of diesel locomotives with few resources available to replace them. In theory, had Britain's economic position been brighter, then main-line electrification might have been an option, but the railways were still perceived as an industry in decline and there was little political will to make the massive investments required. If the railways failed to invest, however, in new high-speed equipment, the industry's position would be further undermined as a result of the massive investment in the country's motorway network and in the growth of domestic air traffic. These constraints led to the design of the prototype High Speed Train at the Railway Technical Centre in Derby. Two power cars — originally numbered 41001 and 41002 (later renumbered 43000 and 43001) — were built at Crewe with the intermediate coaches being constructed at Derby Litchurch Lane.

Designed to operate at high speed on existing lines, the success of the unit on trial led to the development of the HST fleet, which revolutionised main-line travel in Britain, following its introduction. The prototype unit, classified Class 252 under the TOPS scheme, was destined to have a relatively short operational life. Introduced in June 1972 it was transferred to departmental work in November 1976, and, following the cessation of this, No 41001 was handed over to the National Railway Museum. One of the routes that was to be transformed by the introduction of the HSTs was the ex-GWR main line from Paddington and, appropriately, the prototype HST is seen here at Paddington while in service on the Western Region.
Harry Luff/Online Transport Archive

British Rail No 87001

The last of the first-generation of 25kV ac electric locomotives designed for use on the West Coast main line, the Class 87s were ordered following the authorisation of the scheme to electrify the route through from Weaver Junction, between Liverpool and Manchester, and Glasgow. A total of 36 locomotives were ultimately produced; the first 36, Nos 87001-87035, were constructed by Crewe Works and delivered in 1973/74 with the final, non-standard

example (No 87101 fitted with thyristor control), being delivered from Crewe in 1977. Nos 87001-35 were initially allocated to Willesden depot where they were rostered primarily to passenger traffic, while No 87101 was based at Crewe for use on freight services. At Privatisation, all 35 members of Class 87/0 passed on lease to Virgin Trains and remained in service pending the introduction of the new Pendolino units. Following the introduction of these units, Virgin's requirements diminished and

withdrawal or transfer to other operators commenced. In November 2005, No 87001 was transferred to the National Collection and two others are also currently preserved in the UK. Following final withdrawal, the other surviving locomotives are scheduled for transfer for operation in Bulgaria. Here, restored to its original Rail Blue livery, but hauling a rake of Virgin-liveried coaching stock, No 87001 passes Headstone Lane on the 14.15 service from Euston to Birmingham on 2 March 2004. *Hugh Ballantyne*